Eastern Theater 1861–65

COMBAT

Union Infantryman
VERSUS
Confederate Infantryman

Ron Field

First published in Great Britain in 2013 by Osprey Publishing,
Midland House, West Way, Botley, Oxford, OX2 0PH, UK
43-01 21st Street, Suite 220B, Long Island City, NY 11101, USA

E-mail: info@ospreypublishing.com

OSPREY PUBLISHING IS PART OF THE OSPREY GROUP

A CIP catalog record for this book is available from the British
Library

Print ISBN: 978 1 78096 927 5
PDF ebook ISBN: 978 1 4728 0476 1
ePub ebook ISBN: 978 1 4728 0477 8

Index by Fionbar Lyons
Typeset in Univers, Sabon and Adobe Garamond Pro
Maps by bounford.com
Artwork by Peter Dennis
Originated by PDQ Media, Bungay, UK
Printed in China through Asia Pacific Offset Ltd

13 14 15 16 17   10 9 8 7 6 5 4 3 2 1

Osprey Publishing is supporting the Woodland Trust, the UK's
leading woodland conservation charity, by funding the dedication
of trees.

www.ospreypublishing.com

Author's acknowledgments

The author wishes to thank the following for their generous
assistance: Jonathan Eaker, Reference Section, Prints and
Photographs Division, Library of Congress; Michelle A. Krowl,
Civil War and Reconstruction Specialist, Manuscript Division,
Library of Congress; James Singewald, Maryland Historical
Society; Mary Ann Schneider, Assistant Curator/Archivist, Texas
Heritage Museum, Hill College; Patrick A. Schroeder, Historian,
Appomattox Court House National Historical Park; Robert
Delap, Department of Rights and Reproductions, The New-York
Historical Society; Michael J. McAfee; Cortland C. Putbrese;
Richard Ricca; William A. Young, Jr.; Beth Trissel; Pat
Churchman; Susan R. Dixon and John D. Whitfield; Richard
O'Sullivan, William B. Bynum, Andy R. Braeunling, Waverly Byth
Adcock, and John Irvine.

Author's note

The text in this book uses the term "African American" when
referring to those of African descent but several contemporary
sources quoted in this work contain words used at the time.
Often these words were used to offend or degrade people, but are
retained in these pages as they tell us something about the ideas
and feelings of those in the past.

Artist's note

Readers may care to note that the original paintings from which
the artwork plates in this book were prepared are available for
private sale. All reproduction copyright whatsoever is retained by
the Publishers. All inquiries should be addressed to:

Peter Dennis, 'Fieldhead', The Park, Mansfield, Nottinghamshire
NG18 2AT, UK, or email magie.h@ntlworld.com

The publishers regret that they can enter into no correspondence
upon this matter.

Editor's note

The following will help in converting measurements referred to in
the text between U.S. customary and metric measurements:
1 mile = 1.6km
1yd = 0.9m
1ft = 0.3m
1in = 2.54cm/25.4mm
1 U.S. liquid pint = 0.5 liters
1lb = 0.45kg

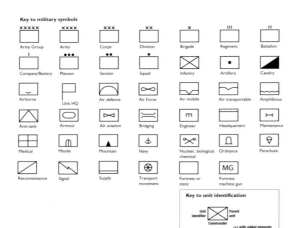

CONTENTS

Introduction

Shells and musket balls crashed through the ranks of the Confederate infantry of Pickett's Division, Army of Northern Virginia, as they advanced with fixed bayonets up the slope towards the Union lines on Cemetery Ridge during the Grand Assault at Gettysburg on July 3, 1863. Behind the stone wall on the ridge, the Union infantry of the 2nd Brigade, Second Division, II Corps, Army of the Potomac, took aim and fired at will. For the men of both armies it was the culmination of long periods of drill and training in preparation for combat. Recruited in the Shenandoah Valley, the 289 men of the 56th Virginia would suffer 65 percent killed, wounded, or missing by the end of that day. One of the regiments waiting behind the stone wall to repulse them, the

Photographed in September of 1862, these Union infantrymen of the 6th Massachusetts Volunteer Militia stand at "parade rest" holding Pattern 1853 Enfield rifle-muskets, of which over 500,000 were purchased from Britain for the Union Army in 1861–63. They are also outfitted with compatible British-made accouterments including a cartridge box containing 50 rounds of ammunition, which is suspended from a plain shoulder belt narrower than its U.S. counterpart. Fastened by a "snake" buckle, the waist belt supports a "Ball Bag" originally used by the British for Brunswick rifle balls but employed by Civil War infantrymen for percussion caps. The bayonet scabbard and "frog" are shaped differently than the U.S. types. (Library of Congress LC-DIG-ppmsca-37124)

U.S. Regular infantrymen are depicted by French artist and engraver André Castaigne attacking the Castle of Chapultepec Castle, home of the Mexican Military Academy, on September 13, 1847, during the Mexican–American War of 1846–48. Young infantry officers serving in this conflict, such as Jefferson Davis, future Confederate president, and Ulysses S. Grant, future commanding general of the Union Army, gained considerable battle experience, which served them well from 1861 through 1865. As colonel of the 1st Mississippi Rifles, the former was one of the first American commanders to use Model 1841 Rifles in combat during the battle of Buena Vista in 1847. As illustrated in the foreground, U.S. infantry officers continued to carry swords into battle in Mexico and did so throughout the Civil War. (Library of Congress, Prints & Photographs Division, LC-USZ62-75569)

71st Pennsylvania, would sustain nearly 40 percent casualties among the 24 officers and 307 enlisted men carried into action at the beginning of the battle. Whether fighting as a raw recruit in the opening campaigns of the 1861, or as a hardened veteran of the Gettysburg or Overland campaigns of 1863 and 1864, the infantryman usually found himself fighting independently, or to use the contemporary term "off his own hook," when engaged in close combat with the enemy. Only then did the true qualities of courage, mixed with a strong survival instinct, blend with drill and training in order to define the infantryman of the Civil War from 1861 through 1865.

The principal arm of combat in the Civil War was infantry. As with all branches of the U.S. military the infantryman had existed for a mere

Shown here are six examples of muzzle-loading long-arms used by Civil War infantrymen. The Model 1855 Springfield rifle-musket (**1**) with Maynard tape-primer magazine was 56in in overall length, weighed approximately 9lb 2oz, fired a .58-caliber Minié ball, and had a minimum effective range of 500yd. Often called "the long-range rifle," the shorter-barreled .58-caliber Model 1855 Harpers Ferry rifle (**2**) was 49.3in overall, weighed 9lb 14oz, and was fitted with a sword bayonet with brass hilt and 21.5in blade. A third-class weapon, the .54-caliber Model 1854 Austrian rifle-musket (**3**) was 52.75in overall, weighed about 7lb 12oz, with a range of about 400yd. Held in similar regard because of its poor range, the .71-caliber M1857 Belgian rifle-musket (**4**) was 56in overall. Used extensively by both the Union and Confederacy, the Pattern 1853 Enfield (**5**) weighed about 8lb 2oz unloaded, and fired a .577-caliber Minié-type ball with a maximum range of about 1,250yd. The .58-caliber Prussian Jaeger rifle (**6**) was 43.8in overall, weighed 9lb 12oz, and had a maximum range of 580yd; it was fitted with a hunting-pattern sword bayonet. (*Official Military Atlas of the Civil War*)

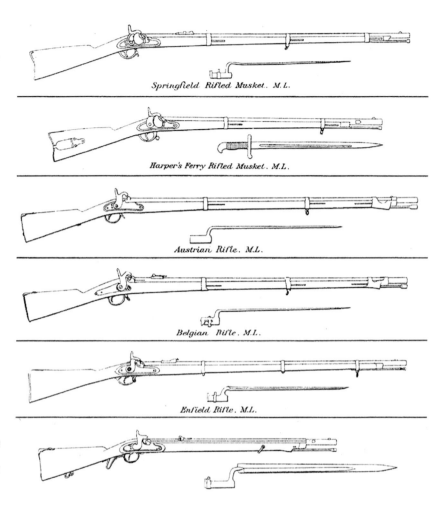

Springfield Rifled Musket. M.L.

Harper's Ferry Rifled Musket. M.L.

Austrian Rifle. M.L.

Belgian Rifle. M.L.

Enfield Rifle. M.L.

86 years when the conflict between the States began. The Revolutionary War of 1775–83 and War of 1812 had seen the birth of the regular American foot soldier and rifleman, supplemented by his militia equivalent. Further conflict with Native Americans during the Black Hawk War of 1831 and the Seminole Wars during the years 1835–58 gave both regulars and militia limited experience fighting guerrilla-style warfare. During that same period the Mexican–American War of 1846–48 had also presented the U.S. infantryman with a more open terrain in which to define his role in battle, although the artillery proved to be the most effective branch of service during that conflict owing to the adoption of modern artillery systems and tactics for the growing U.S. Army during the 1830s. At the beginning of the Civil War in 1861 there were but ten regular infantry regiments in the U.S. Army, and they were largely stationed out West, scattered by companies over thousands of miles. Many of their officers had served in the Mexican–American War, but few had commanded any sizable body of troops. Moreover, although a small number had kept abreast of world

military developments after their services south of the border they were not in a position to dictate policy in Washington, D.C.

The American militia system in existence by 1861 had been created by the Federal Militia Act of May 8, 1792, entitled "An Act More effectively to provide for the National Defence [sic] by establishing a uniform Militia throughout the United States." This act stipulated that "every free able bodied white male citizen of the respective states" from 18 to 45, with certain exceptions, should be enrolled in a militia company in his district within 12 months. Although this system of citizen soldiery had been permitted to deteriorate in many states by the mid-19th century, it had been much revived by 1861, particularly in the Southern states following the John Brown Raid on Harper's Ferry, Virginia, in October of 1859, which threatened the very existence of slavery. Nevertheless, most militiamen in North and South were totally unprepared for the approaching war, being more used to picnics, target shoots, and military balls than campaign and battle. The wide use of this part-time soldiery, plus masses of volunteers, carried with it an inevitable lack of discipline. Citizens temporarily turned soldiers had little sense of unquestioning obedience to higher ranks. Moreover, they almost always elected their own officers, which did not make for stern authority.

The difficult terrain and wooded lands of the Eastern Theater of the Civil War would emphasize the importance of the foot soldier and help relegate cavalry, if not artillery, to lesser tactical roles. In late 1862, Union Col David H. Strother wrote, "I have observed in this war that the fire of infantry is our main dependence in battle." The main infantry weapon at the commencement of hostilities was the smoothbore musket with a maximum effective range of only about 150yd. Hence, the use of massed volley fire was the only way to compensate for a lack of range and accuracy, and resulted in troops advancing in close-order formation of either line or column. Defenders usually stood in line formation and returned volley fire. Mass infantry charges could overwhelm an enemy defensive position, but at great loss of life.

The role of the infantryman would change as advances in technology introduced more accurate and deadlier weapons, while developments in tactics altered the way the foot soldier performed in battle. The rifle-musket began to replace the smoothbore in U.S. service in 1855. Although rifled weapons were not new, being carried by the Regiment of Mounted Riflemen and many state rifle corps, loading them prior to the advent of the rifle-musket was a slow process. The invention of the Minié ball by French Army officer Claude-Etienne Minié, and perfected by James H. Burton, master armorer at Harper's Ferry, meant that rifled weapons could be loaded and fired faster than smoothbores because the ball was dropped down the barrel but expanded into the rifled grooves when the weapon was fired, making it a far more accurate weapon. Spinning out of the barrel, the ball remained on target for at least 500yd. This increased accuracy was to have a marked effect on the performance of the infantryman on the Civil War battlefield, and

The infantry clashes explored in this book took place in three main theaters of operation during the Civil War. Very much a result of Northern clamor for a rapid advance on the Confederate capital of Richmond, Virginia, the battle of First Bull Run/Manassas on July 21, 1861, ended with the rout and retreat of Brig Gen Irwin McDowell's Union Army of Northeastern Virginia back to Washington, D.C. The Confederate invasion of Pennsylvania by the Army of Northern Virginia, under Gen Robert E. Lee, led to a collision with Maj Gen George G. Meade's Army of the Potomac at Gettysburg on July 1, 1863. On the third day of battle, Lee ordered Pickett's/ Pettigrew's/Trimble's charge, which failed to break through the Union defenses on Cemetery Ridge and resulted in Confederate defeat and withdrawal back into Virginia. During the siege of Richmond/Petersburg in 1864, African American troops of Maj Gen Benjamin Butler's Army of the James spearheaded an attack on defenses south of the Confederate capital at Chaffin's Farm/New Market Heights on September 29, 1864, which earned white officers and African American enlisted men a total of 14 Medals of Honor. Each of these encounters highlights the courage and tenacity of the infantryman in combat during the Civil War.

Developed by French Army officers Claude-Etienne Minié and Henri-Gustave Delvigne, the Minié ball had a hollow base and three ring bands that expanded into the rifling inside the musket barrel upon firing, as illustrated in this diagram from an 1856 U.S. publication, which indicates it was suitable for arms altered from smoothbore to rifled muskets. (*Reports of Experiments with Small Arms*)

tactics began to favor the defending infantry, which increasingly made use of breastworks and field fortifications.

However, as the Civil War unfolded, attacking forces were not necessarily mown down before they arrived in near proximity of an enemy armed with rifled weapons, but – due to the effect of black-powder smoke, which obscured visibility – often managed to get within close range, where they exchanged fire until ammunition was expended. Furthermore, improved weaponry did not necessarily cause armies to dig field fortifications. This development was encouraged more by the education received at the U.S. Military Academy at West Point, New York, where every prospective officer in the pre-war Army attended courses in engineering conducted by Professor Dennis Hart Mahan. Despite advances in tactics and technology, and rigid textbook training, the infantryman in close combat inevitably fought independently, and "off his own hook," throughout the Civil War as the din of battle and loss of leadership took its toll. Thus, survival and success were dependent on personal courage, and on the drill and training received in preparation for battle.

BALL FOR ALTERED MUSKET.

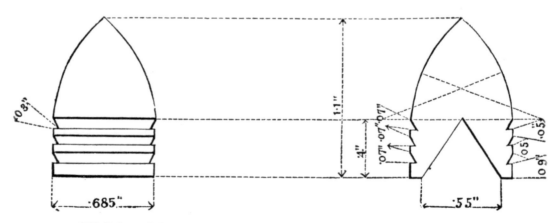

Weight of ball, 730 grains; weight of powder, 70 grains.

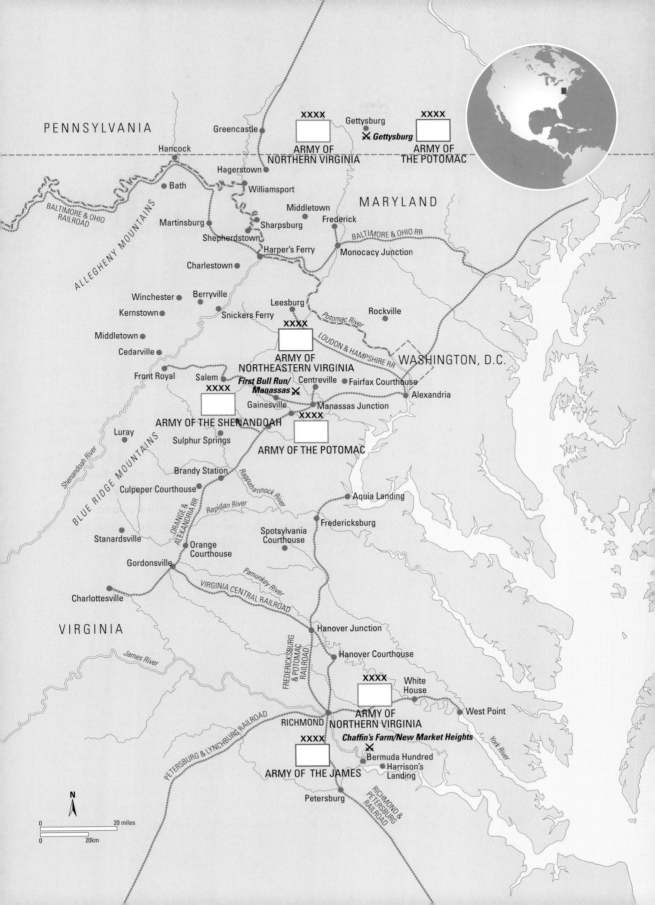

PENNSYLVANIA

Greencastle   Gettysburg

Hancock   Gettysburg

XXXX
ARMY OF
NORTHERN VIRGINIA

XXXX
ARMY OF
THE POTOMAC

Hagerstown

Bath

Williamsport

MARYLAND

Middletown

Martinsburg   Sharpsburg   Frederick

BALTIMORE & OHIO
RAILROAD

Shepherdstown

BALTIMORE & OHIO RR

Harper's Ferry   Monocacy Junction

Charlestown

Winchester   Berryville   Leesburg   Rockville

Kernstown   Snickers Ferry   Potomac River

Middletown

XXXX
ARMY OF
NORTHEASTERN VIRGINIA

LOUDON & HAMPSHIRE RR

WASHINGTON, D.C.

Cedarville

Front Royal   Salem   First Bull Run/
Manassas   Centreville   Fairfax Courthouse

Alexandria

XXXX   Gainesville   Manassas Junction

ARMY OF THE SHENANDOAH

XXXX
ARMY OF THE POTOMAC

Luray

Sulphur Springs

Shenandoah River

BLUE RIDGE MOUNTAINS

Brandy Station

Culpeper Courthouse   Aquia Landing

Rappahannock River

ORANGE & ALEXANDRIA RR

Rapidan River   Fredericksburg

Stanardsville   Spotsylvania
Courthouse

Orange
Courthouse

Gordonsville

Pamunkey River

Charlottesville   VIRGINIA CENTRAL RAILROAD

VIRGINIA

Hanover Junction

James River

FREDERICKSBURG & POTOMAC RAILROAD

Hanover Courthouse

XXXX   White
House

ARMY OF
NORTHERN VIRGINIA   West Point

RICHMOND

Chaffin's Farm/New Market Heights

XXXX   Bermuda Hundred

Harrison's
Landing   York River

ARMY OF THE JAMES

PETERSBURG & LYNCHBURG RAILROAD

RICHMOND & PETERSBURG RAILROAD

Petersburg

N

0   20 miles
0   20km

ALLEGHENY MOUNTAINS

The Opposing Sides

BUILDING AN ARMY

Union

On April 15, 1861, President Abraham Lincoln called for 75,000 three-month militia, all of which were to be infantry with the exception of three companies of cavalry. On May 3, Lincoln asked for 42,034 three-year volunteers and 22,714 regulars. On July 22, the day after First Bull Run/Manassas, Congress authorized a volunteer force of a further 500,000 men including cavalry and artillery. Further calls for volunteers were made throughout the remainder of the war with varying degrees of success. Many of those who enlisted or re-enlisted for longer terms of service quickly succumbed to disease or exposure, meaning that by 1863 the Union infantryman was a hardier breed of soldier.

Following the decimation of the Union Army through casualties, expiration of enlistment, and desertion, Congress enacted the Enrolment Act of March 3, 1863, which was the first instance of mass conscription in U.S. history, and aimed to raise an army of 300,000. This required the enrollment of every male citizen and those immigrants who had filed for citizenship aged between 20 and 45. However, 86,724 drafted men achieved exemption from military service via a payment of $300 each. A further 75,429 conscripts paid substitutes to take their place in the ranks of the Union Army. This inequality resulted in the Draft Riots of 1864, and the Civil War came to be regarded as a rich man's war and a poor man's fight.

Orders issued on April 15, 1861 for volunteer forces mustered into Federal service, and consolidated by General Orders No. 15, dated May 4, 1861, called for an infantry regiment to be made up of ten companies. The regimental staff was to include a colonel, lieutenant colonel, major, adjutant (with the rank of lieutenant), regimental quartermaster (a lieutenant), assistant surgeon, sergeant major, regimental quartermaster sergeant, regimental commissary sergeant, hospital steward, drum major and fife major, plus 24 regimental bandsmen. Regimental bands were officially abolished in July of 1862, although some regiments were able to retain their bands after that time by re-enlisting the musicians as combatants and then detailing them to the band. Also authorized via General Orders No. 15, the regimental chaplain held no command rank but instead entered the army with the rank of private.

The ten companies were lettered A through K; the letter J was not used, however, because it was too like the letter I. Each infantry company consisted of one captain, one first lieutenant, and one second lieutenant (initially called an "ensign"), five sergeants, eight corporals, one drummer, one fifer, one wagoner, plus a maximum of 101 and a minimum of 64 privates. Each infantry company was divided into two platoons of approximately 30–50 men, which in turn were subdivided into sections of about 15–30 men. Sections were subdivided into squads of about 8–16 men. The ranking enlisted man, the first sergeant, "ran the company," writing reports, taking musters and keeping records. The second, third, fourth, and fifth sergeants commanded a section each. Squads were commanded by corporals. Dependent on which drill book was followed, squads could be divided into two-man or four-man skirmish groups, the latter being termed "comrades in battle."

Regardless of General Orders, the size of Union volunteer regiments was not standardized and they frequently began their campaigning with well over 1,000 men each and organized into more than ten companies. The 71st Pennsylvania Volunteer Infantry, or "Old California Regiment," consisted of 1,500 men divided into three battalions of five companies each, but was reduced to a ten-company regiment in August 1861 (Vanderslice 1978: 29).

However, an almost universal rule was that before many months had passed about one fifth of the men in most regiments had vanished from the ranks in various ways. Some died of disease or exhaustion, and as many more were discharged for physical disability. Absenteeism was caused by sickness, or by those feigning sickness. Others were detailed for special duty as bakers, wagon drivers, tailors, cobblers, or hospital nurses, as the logistical demands of the army demanded specialist skills. For example, Co. K, 71st Pennsylvania originally enlisted 94 men on June 28, 1861, but at Gettysburg on July 3, 1863, this company fielded only 19 men, which included all ranks.

Entitled "Volunteers on the march to Charleston," this engraving was published in the *New York Illustrated News* on April 20, 1861. The enlisted men are holding their muskets at "Right shoulder shift," while the officer salutes with his sword. Many of these infantrymen went on to serve the Confederate cause in Virginia. (Author's collection)

Published in the *Daily Chronicle* of New London, Connecticut, on April 18, 1861, this "Rally to the Flag" notice was intended to inspire the local male population to enlist for three months' service in the 1st Connecticut Volunteer Infantry to defend the nation against "Rebellion and Treason." (Author's collection)

Confederate

The first infantry to eventually form part of the Confederate Army consisted of volunteers from the militia and independent volunteer companies of South Carolina, who enlisted for 12 months' state service in response to the call issued by Governor Francis Pickens on December 17, 1860. Similar movements were begun in the lower South states of Mississippi, Florida, Alabama, Georgia, Louisiana, and Texas, and on February 28, 1861, these troops were accepted into the Confederate Provisional Army, within which they completed that period of service, thus creating an army of 100,000 men. Established by Act of Confederate Congress on March 6, 1861, the Regular Army of the Confederate States of America was intended to consist of 10,600 men, but never achieved that level. Hence, the bulk of the Confederate fighting force was composed of the infantry of the Provisional Army.

When the Civil War began, Confederate President Jefferson Davis called for about 60,000 volunteers for 12 months' service by mid-April 1861. Following the secession of the Upper South states of Virginia, Arkansas, Tennessee, and North Carolina that year, Congress authorized a "reserved army corps" of 30,000 men for emergency service as needed. On February 2, 1862, the President called for 500,000 troops "for the war." On April 16 of the same year Congress approved the Conscription Act, which authorized Davis to draft all white males aged between 18 and 35 years with substitutes permitted. At the same time the terms of all men already in service were extended to three years. On February 17, 1864, Congress authorized the establishment of reserve forces for state defense. These troops were organized at various times thereafter. Finally, on March 13, 1865, the Confederacy accepted African American slaves as soldiers, who were to be freed if the Southern cause prevailed.

As with Union troops, Confederate regiments started out with full ranks which were depleted as the war took its toll. For example, the 1st Virginia Volunteer Infantry consisted of 642 officers and men on August 31, 1861, but by the same date in 1863 it had a total strength of only 110. The last muster roll for this regiment, completed on August 31, 1864, contained 178 names, which reflected an average strength of 29 men for each of its six remaining

Entitled "The War Excitement in New York: Scene in Front of a Fire-Engine House" and published on May 25, 1861, this engraving based on a sketch by Thomas Nast shows a crowd gathered in front of several large posters which denounce the Confederacy and call all firemen of the city to arms. (*Illustrated London News*)

companies. From an original mustered strength of 573, the 11th Georgia Volunteer Infantry fielded only 140 at Sharpsburg/Antietam having lost many men to illness during the winter of 1861/62. After replenishing its ranks with recruits and conscripts, it sustained a total of 310 killed, wounded, and missing at Gettysburg, amounting to 65 percent of its total number. When this regiment surrendered at Appomattox in 1865 it amounted to only 16 officers and 176 enlisted men.

RECRUITING INFANTRY

Union

The volunteers of 1861 were motivated by speeches and rallying cries given by future commanders such as Benjamin Butler, who addressed those gathering in Essex County, Massachusetts, on April 19, saying "Let us swear as we love our mothers, as we love our sisters, and honor our fathers, as we hope for heaven hereafter, to maintain inviolate the union of these States" (*BDA* Apr 20, 1861: 2:3). Editorials and notices in local newspapers appealed to men to join companies being recruited in cities, townships, and local communities with phrases such as "Rally to the Flag." Volunteers were also encouraged to enlist via the aid of recruiting posters. Recruiting parties scoured the back streets of the major cities. Although some volunteers enlisted to prove their masculinity to their peers rather than from any deep-seated feeling of patriotism, many men were physically ill prepared for the forthcoming campaigns, although medical examination was minimal. Although the three-month volunteers were

Many African American freedmen, and even some slaves, at least outwardly supported the Confederacy at the beginning of the Civil War. Entitled "Recruiting for the Confederate Army at Woodstock, Virginia," this engraving was published in *Harper's Weekly* on October 5, 1861. (Author's collection)

This Southern handbill encourages the men of Morristown, Tennessee, "To Arms" by enlisting in an infantry company to defend their state and the Confederacy. The Secession cockade was worn by Pvt G.F. Campbell who enlisted in the Liberty Guards (Co. L), 10th South Carolina Volunteer Infantry. He was one of five men in his regiment to die of disease while encamped on Cat Island, Winyah Bay, South Carolina, during the summer of 1861. (Author's collection)

inspired by the cause for which they fought, their morale was often low due to their treatment by the Federal government. Poor rations were a major cause of discontent. Pvt Phillip W. Hudson of the 1st Connecticut Volunteer Infantry wrote from Camp Buckingham on May 17, 1861: "We have been obliged to go without some meals on account of their being so bad … I have not eaten a ration since we have been in camp." Buying all his food from free African Americans and slaves who came into camp morning and night, he concluded, "They are very reasonable in their prices, and as long as our money lasts we shall live well, and no thanks to government officers" (*HDC* May 22, 1861: 2:3).

Confederate

Most of the infantry raised in South Carolina in January of 1861 were recruited from the beat, or non-uniformed, militia who were required to meet at their local muster ground and volunteer for state service either as individuals or as an entire company. Accepted as volunteer companies, they elected their officers, as in the Union Army.

Motivation for enlistment throughout the rest of the Deep South was unequivocal in its defense of States' Rights and slavery. At a meeting of the Scott Rifles (named for Lt Gen Winfield Scott) of Talbotton, Georgia, on January 8, 1861, Pvt William A. Little stated:

We believe that South Carolina "is, and of right ought to be, free"; and, connected with her as we are, by blood, by climate and by soil … [we] support the same institutions, and defend the same rights, manifestly the friends of South Carolina are our friends – her hopes are our hopes – her enemies are our enemies – her destiny our destiny. Therefore be it. (*CDT* Jan 25, 1861: 2:2)

On this occasion the Scott Rifles changed their name to the Southern Rifles in repudiation of the Northern general's "proposed plan of a campaign against the Southern States." The Southern Rifles became Co. A, 4th Georgia Volunteer Infantry, and served in Northern Virginia throughout the war.

UNIFORMS, EQUIPMENT, AND WEAPONS

Union

A lack of uniformity in clothing among Union volunteers caused much confusion during the early part of the war. Three-month volunteers from the Northern states were further demoralized upon receipt of poorly made uniforms and inferior arms. Much of the clothing and footwear failed to stand up to the rigors of the Manassas Campaign. Recalling its period of encampment at Martinsburg, Virginia, July 8–15, 1861, Stephen Abbott, regimental historian of the 1st New Hampshire Volunteer Infantry, wrote, "The clothes of the men, which were poor at best, had become much worn, and they were almost shoeless." An inspector sent by Governor Curtin found the 4th and 5th Pennsylvania Volunteer Infantry at Washington, D.C., to be "suffering greatly," with blouses and pants of "all colors, and made of damaged goods of inferior quality, mostly of 'shoddy' and some of 'Kentucky jean'" (*PI* May 28, 1861: 8:4).

Many volunteers supplemented their long arm with side arms. A private in Co. A, 11th New York Volunteer Infantry (1st Fire Zouaves), and personal secretary to the first regimental commander, Col Elmer Ellsworth, Arthur O'Neil Alcock wrote that many of his fellow Zouaves carried revolvers and had "knives stuck in their belts," which supplemented their Sharps rifles and sword bayonets, as they boarded the steamer *Baltic* bound for Annapolis, Maryland. Dissatisfied with their rifles, which they considered unsuitable for Zouaves, the 11th New York received Model 1855 rifle-muskets – although the two flank companies (A and K) continued to carry Model 1855 rifles with sword bayonets.

LEFT
Much confusion was caused in battle by Union infantrymen wearing gray and Confederate infantrymen clothed in blue. Dressed in a gray uniform, Pvt Humphrey Blaisdell, Jr. enlisted in the Gymnasium Company (Co. G), 2nd Maine Volunteer Infantry, and was wounded in the leg and captured at First Bull Run/Manassas on July 21, 1861. Following exchange and further war service he was appointed first lieutenant, Co. K, 12th U.S. Colored Heavy Artillery on July 23, 1864. (Author's collection)

CENTER
In this digitally enhanced image, Pvt James W. Bare, West Augusta Guard (Co. L), 5th Virginia Volunteer Infantry, wears the blue militia uniform based on Virginia State regulations of 1858, which in turn were influenced by Federal regulations. His waist and shoulder belts are of white buff leather which was quite common among ante-bellum militia units. Bare was mortally wounded at Winchester, Virginia, on September 19, 1864. At First Bull Run/Manassas, blue-coated troops of the 33rd Virginia were mistaken for Union infantrymen by Ricketts' battery with fatal consequences for the artillerists. (Cortland C. Putbrese collection)

RIGHT
Garibaldian-style red shirts like the one worn by this unidentified infantryman were worn as a basic uniform by many units in both Union and Confederate armies during the first few months of war. This enlisted man holds a Model 1842 smoothbore musket. (Author's collection)

This plate depicts an enlisted man of the 71st Pennsylvania, 2nd Brigade ("Philadelphia Brigade"), Second Division, II Corps, stooped in the "aim" position and about to fire over a breastwork formed by stacking wooden rails and fence posts on top of the low stone wall at "The Bloody Angle" on Cemetery Ridge at Gettysburg. Ready for immediate use, several loaded rifle-muskets lean against the stone wall. The figure is based on Pvt George Washington Beidelman, Co. C, 71st Pennsylvania, who was slightly wounded in the leg during this action.

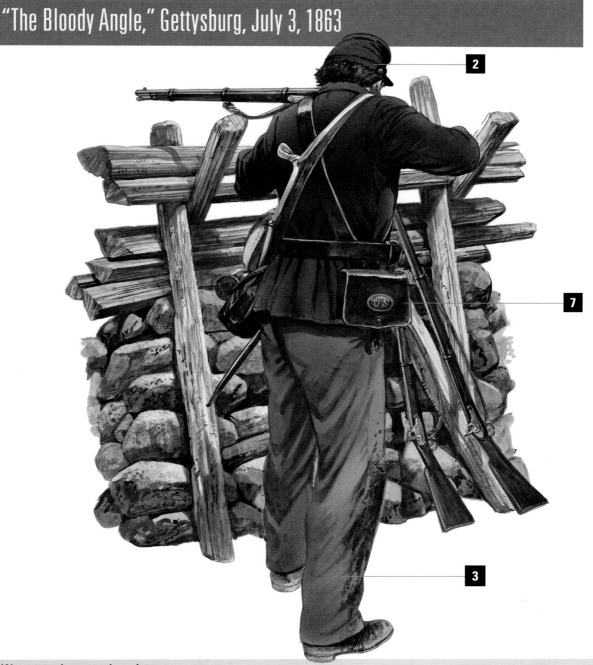

Weapons, dress, and equipment

Like most soldiers of the Union Army, the men of the 71st Pennsylvania wore dark-blue, four-button woolen sack coats (**1**) and wool broadcloth forage caps (**2**) with sky-blue woolen pants (**3**). A small flannel-cloth, blue trefoil II Corps badge (**4**) is sewn to the top of his cap. Compared with that of his Confederate counterpart, his footwear (**5**) is in good condition.

He is armed with a Model 1861 Springfield rifle-musket (**6**) weighing approximately 9lb unloaded, which fired a .58-caliber Minié ball. It had a maximum range of about 500yd, and an effective range of up to 300yd. Accouterments consist of a Pattern 1861 leather cartridge box

(**7**) suspended from a shoulder belt bearing a round "eagle plate" (**8**); it weighed 4lb when fully loaded with 40 rounds of ammunition. As with the Confederates, he also has a pouch for percussion caps (**9**). Water is carried in a cloth-covered tin canteen (**10**) with a capacity of 3 pints, while rations plus extra ammunition are held in an oil-cloth haversack (**11**); nine or ten pieces of hardtack, hard bread shaped like a cracker, represented a day's ration. His painted canvas knapsack containing personal belongings, plus a blanket, has been removed prior to battle action. Without the knapsack, the entire weight of his weapon and equipment amounted to 30lb.

Confederate

As a result of the commutation system established by the Confederate government in February of 1861, volunteers of the Provisional Army were originally to provide their own clothing, for which they would receive $25 every six months. This was supplemented until at least 1862 by uniform supplies from state government and volunteer aid societies. Organized in hundreds of Southern towns and hamlets by local womenfolk, the latter raised funds, bought materials, and made coats, jackets, pants, and shirts for infantry in the front line. Although gray predominated, uniforms of many other colors were worn. With the establishment of the first Quartermaster Clothing Bureau in Richmond, Virginia, during the fall of 1861, some volunteers began to receive quartermaster-issue uniforms consisting of gray "roundabouts," or jackets, and gray or sky-blue pants, with gray caps, or hats of various hues. By the beginning of 1863, most Confederate volunteer infantry within supply range of a C.S. clothing depot were in receipt of this type of uniform.

In its early stages the Confederacy had great trouble with the endless variety of arms and calibers in use by its forces, with scarcely 10 percent of its long arms being the .58-caliber rifle-musket at that time the regulation weapon for U.S. infantry. By mid-1863 the commonest arms in General Robert E. Lee's Army of Northern Virginia were the .577-caliber and .58-caliber rifle-muskets including the U.S. Model 1861; the Richmond copy of the U.S. Model 1855 musket; and the British Long Enfield (Tower) musket. Next in importance were smoothbore and a few rifle-muskets of .69 caliber. Third in importance were the .54-caliber Mississippi and similar rifles. Later in the war, a limited number of unusual rifles were used by Confederate infantry, including captured Whitworth and Sharps rifles.

Both of these enlisted men wear quartermaster-issue uniforms, of which most Confederate infantrymen were in receipt by 1863. The man at top wears a second-pattern jacket. His infantry "I" buttons can clearly be seen. The man below wears a third-pattern jacket, minus shoulder straps, and holds a single-shot pistol. (Library of Congress DIG-ppmsca-37175 & DIG-ppmsca-37171)

DRILL MANUALS AND TACTICS

Union

The drill manuals used by the Union Army and militia throughout the U.S.A. prior to the Civil War consisted of *Infantry-Tactics or Rules for the Exercise and Manoeuvres of the United States' Infantry*, published in 1835 and slightly revised in 1839, and *Hardee's Rifle and Light Infantry Tactics for the Exercise and Manoeuvres of Troops when acting as Light Infantry or Riflemen*, published in 1855. The former was a faithful translation by Winfield Scott of the French drill book, which had been modernized in 1831, and was published in three volumes, the first of which dealt with the "manual of arms," or the training of the individual soldier, plus company movements such as marching and firing in line. Volume Two covered battalion, or regimental, drill and the role of the skirmisher. The third volume addressed brigade- and divisional-scale maneuver. Due to its slow standard rate of march (80 steps per minute) and the fact that it did not employ doubling and un-doubling of files, Scott's *Infantry-Tactics* had lost much of its influence by 1861. With the exception of the third volume dealing with the movement of brigades and divisions, it had been replaced by Hardee's *Rifle and Light Infantry Tactics*.

Influenced by the doctrines of the French *chasseurs à pied*, or foot rifles, and published in two volumes, Hardee's *Tactics* was written by William J. Hardee while serving as tactics instructor at West Point in 1853–54, and was designed for use with the 33in-barreled Model 1841 rifle with sword bayonet. As opposed to Scott's slow and cumbersome heavy infantry tactics, the maneuvers of Hardee's, known as the "shanghai drill," were to be conducted at "common time" of 90 steps per minute, and a "gymnastic" pace, or "double quick" of 165–180 steps per minute, which meant infantry could travel over 150yd per minute, given a relatively flat terrain with no undergrowth or fences in the way. Of special importance in this context was the movement from column into "line of battle" and back into column while on the march. Once in "line of battle" and engaged with the enemy, a regiment was committed and its options dramatically reduced. Another one of Hardee's innovations was a system of "comrades in battle" consisting of a group of four soldiers, adjacent to each other in rank and file. Created primarily for skirmish action, they were drilled to work together as a team.

Unfortunately, the Model 1841 rifle was never issued in the numbers envisioned. The pre-war militia, and indeed most of the U.S. Army, continued to use the 42in-barrel smoothbore musket or 40in-barrel rifle-musket, both of which were fitted with socket bayonets. During the first 18 months of the Civil War the Union Army, under an order of May 1, 1861, used an exact reprint of Hardee's revised manual, which did not, however, mention his name as he had resigned from the U.S. Army in January of that year, and was commissioned a colonel in the Confederate Army (see below). Other drill

These figures from Vol. 1 of Silas Casey's three-volume *Infantry Tactics*, published by the Union Army on August 11, 1862, illustrate the drill positions "Shoulder arms," "Support arms," "Fire," and "Guard against infantry." (Casey's *Infantry Tactics*, 1862)

This plate depicts an infantryman of the 56th Virginia, Garnett's Brigade, Pickett's Division, Army of Northern Virginia, as he would have looked during Pickett's charge on July 3, 1863. His division had marched, and then run, 2,000yd across an undulating plain under enemy artillery and musketry fire. As they approached the stone wall at what became known as "The Bloody Angle" on Cemetery Ridge, they were ordered to "charge bayonets," following which every man fought "off his own hook."

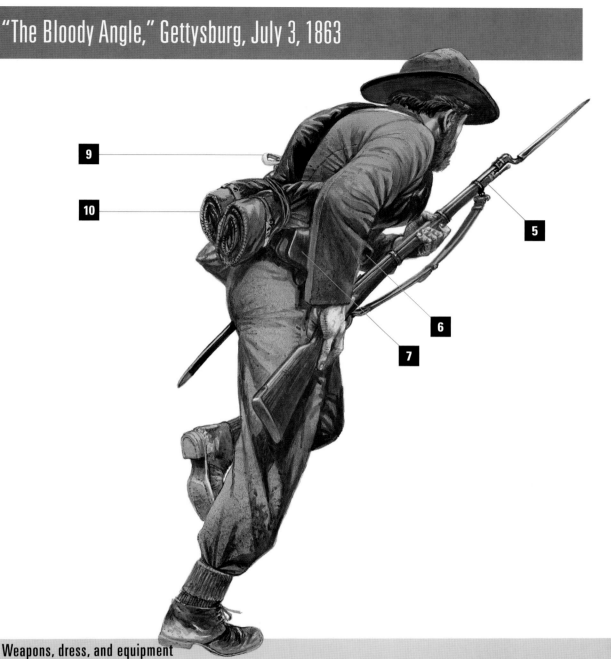

Weapons, dress, and equipment

This soldier wears C.S. quartermaster-issue clothing consisting of a gray jacket (**1**) and sky-blue pants (**2**), plus brown slouch hat (**3**) and Army shoes or bootees (**4**), all of which are much worn. He is armed with a Pattern 1853 Enfield rifle-musket (**5**) weighing about 9lb 8oz unloaded; it fired a .577-caliber Minié-type ball and offered an effective range of up to 500yd, and maximum range of about 900yd. By 1863 the Confederacy had purchased about 400,000 Enfields from various British sources.

His equipment consists of a leather cap pouch (**6**) attached to his waist belt on the right hip, containing copper percussion caps, and a Pattern 1861 cartridge box (**7**), which was designed to carry 40 rounds of elongated Minié balls. Water was carried in either wooden or tin

drum canteens, although some men captured Northern-made Model 1858 tin bull's-eye canteens, which carried a maximum of 3 pints of liquid. This man carries a wooden drum canteen (**8**), which had a capacity of about 2½ pints.

Most men deliberately shortened the straps (**9**) on their equipment so that it sat at waist height and did not bang on their hip. Although some carried knapsacks, others preferred a blanket roll wrapped in a waterproof gum blanket (**10**), which also served as a shelter half which two men combined together to make a shelter tent. Each man in Pickett's division carried three days' rations in his haversack; these rations had been issued during the evening before the action. The weight of his rifle-musket and equipment amounted to about 30lb.

manuals based on Hardee's revised tactics were also published in 1860–63. These included *The Zouave Drill, being a Complete Manual of Arms for the use of The Rifled Musket*, produced by Col Elmer E. Ellsworth in 1861, which was used by several Northern Zouave regiments, including the 11th New York at First Bull Run/Manassas.

As Hardee's drill did not provide for the movement of brigade and division, and Scott's third volume was outdated, the Union Army adopted Maj Gen Silas Casey's three-volume system of *Infantry Tactics* on August 11, 1862. Although Vols 1 and 2 retained Hardee's drill for the individual soldier, company, and battalion, Vol. 3 replaced Scott's obsolete brigade manual. Produced for the benefit of newly promoted United States Colored Troops (USCT) company-grade officers, most of whom had been noncommissioned officers in white regiments and had trained according to different manuals, *Casey's U.S. Infantry Tactics for Colored Troops* was published on March 9, 1863.

None of these manuals made much of hand-to-hand fighting, which the Civil War infantryman sometimes had to contend with in combat. Bayonet drill was confined to two movements in Hardee's *Tactics*, i.e. "Guard against infantry" and "Guard against cavalry," and this was used in training far more often than target practice with live rounds, presumably in order to preserve ammunition. However, ambitious U.S. Army engineer 1/Lt (later Maj Gen) George McClellan had translated a

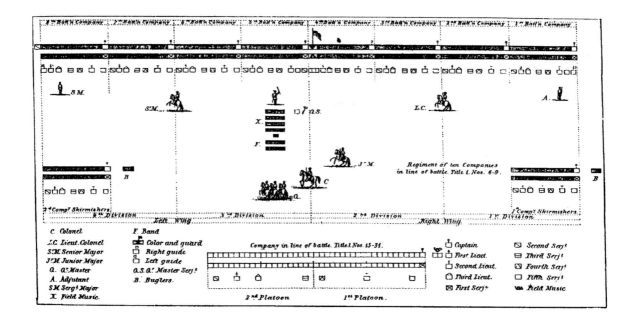

French bayonet-fencing manual in 1852, and several alternative systems were available. Very formalized with correct posture and sprightly footwork for both thrusting and parrying, these drills were dependent on the enemy being willing to engage in fencing with his bayonet. In reality, the Civil War infantryman was more likely to fire his musket or use its butt as a club when fighting at close quarters, than to engage in choreographed bayonet fencing. Bayonets were fixed in battle only when the order to charge was imminent: to fix them sooner would interfere with loading and firing. Commenting on the war in late 1862, Union Col David H. Strother wrote, "There has been no bayonet charge from either side that amounted to anything" (quoted in Eby 1961: 119).

Clearly being drilled with Hardee's *Tactics*, a Massachusetts volunteer wrote from Washington, D.C., on May 17, 1861: "We are getting to rather prefer 'double-quick' time for a two mile march to the slow-measured tread of common time. It is a famous pastime in battalion drill to charge down a ravine on one side, and up on the other in double-quick, imagining a fort at the top of the hill which we immediately take" (*BDA* May 22, 1861: 2:3). Although the Union Army adopted Hardee's *Tactics*, when it came to the real thing, most of its infantry regiments did not use the "double-quick" for anything other than short periods, and the advanced *chasseur* theory it propounded, plus other forms of "Zouave" drill, generally failed to materialize.

Confederate

Not content to use existing copies of pre-war U.S. Army tactics and drill manuals, publishers throughout the South adapted and produced numerous

Published in 1862, this plate shows an infantry regiment of ten companies in "line of battle" with the two flank companies posted as skirmishers. Inset at bottom center is a single company also in "line of battle" formation. (Casey's *Infantry Tactics*, 1862)

OPPOSITE
A plate from *Skirmishers' Drill and Bayonet Exercise* by Lt Col Richard M. Cary, published in Richmond, Virginia, in 1861, which was largely based on McClellan's *Manual of Bayonet Exercise* of 1852. In reality, the Civil War infantryman was more likely to fire his musket or use its butt as a club when fighting at close quarters, than to engage in choreographed bayonet fencing. (Author's collection)

texts for the Confederate infantryman during the conflict. On leave in Georgia when his home state seceded, William J. Hardee resigned from the U.S. Army and was commissioned a colonel in the Confederate Army. In May of 1861 he produced a revised and improved edition of his *Tactics*, including a manual of arms for the three-band musket; this edition was published in Mobile, Alabama, with various other editions appearing later in the war.

Other drill manuals used by Confederate forces included *A System for Conducting Musketry Instruction* by Calhoun Benham, which was prepared and printed in Richmond, Virginia, in 1863 by order of Gen Braxton Bragg, Army of the Tennessee. In part a copy of the 1859 "Regulations for Conducting the Musketry Instruction" used by the British Army, and most suited for the Enfield rifle and rifle-musket, with which a large part of the Confederate Army was armed, this volume included the importance of individual musketry instruction for effective use with rifled arms. Adapted to "Hardee's Drill," by Col John H. Richardson, an officer in the C.S. Provisional Army, *Infantry Tactics, or, Rules for the Exercise and Manœuvres of the Confederate States Infantry* was the Confederate version of Scott's third volume, specifically designed for use with troop formations and maneuvers above battalion level.

The *Skirmishers' Drill and Bayonet Exercise*, as used by the French Army and compiled for "the Use of the Volunteers of the State of Virginia and the South" by Lt Col Richard M. Cary, was published in Richmond, Virginia, in 1861, and was largely based on McClellan's *Manual of Bayonet Exercise* of 1852. As instructor of Tactics and Commandant of Cadets at

JUST RECEIVED
A fresh supply of
HARDEE'S TACTICS,
With the addition of a
"MANUEL FOR COLTS' PISTOL."
New Southern Edition.
TWO VOLS. CLOTH. Price $2.50.
Sent by mail on receipt of $2.75. Send on your orders immediately, before the supply is exhausted.
J. W. BURKE, Agent.
Macon, July 2d, 1861.

New Edition of Hardee's Tactics.
Revised by Col. HARDEE, and
PUBLISHED IN MOBILE.
Price $2.50. Two Volumes Illustrated.
Mailed for $2.75 to any part of the State.
Also, a few fine LITHOGRAPH MAPS of the Seat of War. Price $3.00. Address
J. W. BURKE, Agent.
July 15, 1861.

the Virginia Military Institute (VMI), Col William Gilham published a Confederate version of his *Manual of Instruction* in 1861 and 1862, which was used by the "Stonewall Brigade" at First Bull Run/Manassas.

A key Confederate infantry tactic not contained within any drill book was the "rebel yell." Used both to scare Union defenders and to reassure Confederate attackers, this was variously described as a high, piercing scream and a series of yips constantly changing in volume and pitch. One of the earliest accounts of its use was on July 21, 1861, when Brig Gen Thomas J. Jackson ordered his brigade to fix bayonets and "yell like furies" as they charged down Henry House Hill during First Bull Run/Manassas.

Photographed at Falmouth, Virginia, on April 24, 1863, the 110th Pennsylvania Volunteer Infantry is formed in "line of battle" standing at "Shoulder arms." The general left guide is visible holding a marker flag on a staff. The color guard is seen left of the center-right company, while the regimental commander stands at left with an orderly holding his horse. Staff officers, probably including the regimental chaplain, stand nearest the camera. (Library of Congress LC-B8184-10415)

CONDUCT IN BATTLE

Both Union and Confederate regiments marched in tightly closed formations, often elbow-to-elbow and usually at brigade or division strength by mid-war, with the Union brigade composed of from four to seven regiments typically numbering about 1,250 and the Union division about 6,000 infantrymen. Confederate brigades and divisions were generally larger, with the former numbering about 1,500 and the latter about 7,000.

Such a large mass of men presented a prominent target for defenders behind breastworks or in rifle pits, who could easily fire several volleys before the enemy would be close enough for hand-to-hand combat. However, such massed attacks often succeeded due to sheer persistence, physical courage and a tactical innovation instituted by the men themselves – that of keeping the enemy's heads down by maintaining a rolling fire while advancing.

Using a new tactic foreshadowing those used in World War I, Col Emory Upton, commanding the 2nd Brigade, First Division, VI Corps, Army of the Potomac, devised a method of attack which penetrated the "Mule Shoe" salient at Spotsylvania Court House on May 10, 1864, wherein columns of massed infantry would swiftly assault and capture a small part of the enemy line without pausing to trade fire. Using the entire II Corps, Maj Gen Winfield S. Hancock adapted Upton's columnar assault tactic to break through at the same point two days later. In the end, the manual was revised, not in writing, but through the bitter experience of the men who had to use it.

During general battlefield maneuver, written orders were carried from the commanding general to brigade and/or regimental commanders by mounted staff officers or enlisted cavalrymen serving as couriers. Field officers then

Infantry regiments in both Union and Confederate armies were drilled to form into "hollow squares" to repel cavalry, as seen in this view of the 139th Pennsylvania Volunteer Infantry. The field officers, color guard and regimental band can be seen inside the double rank of infantrymen with fixed bayonets. During the first day at Gettysburg, the Confederate infantry were forced to halt their advance and form squares when Buford's cavalry feinted as if preparing to charge. (Library of Congress LC-B8184-B306)

issued commands to battalion and company commanders who passed them down to the enlisted infantrymen. In battle it was hard for officers and NCOs to control infantry fire. Verbal commands were difficult to hear during the din and chaos of battle and, if they had not been sent to the rear to serve as stretcher bearers or runners, field musicians helped relay orders. The leading drummer and fifer were posted on the right of the field music. In view of both the colonel and lieutenant colonel, the drummers and buglers could alert the troops to an upcoming movement via a series of "calls" which included *Quick Time*, *Double Quick Time*, *Halt*, *Commence Firing*, *Cease Firing*, and *Retreat*. Early-war regiments' flank companies, which specialized in skirmish duty, often had buglers even when most of the regiment's musicians were drummers and fifers, and throughout the war buglers, if present, accompanied companies on the skirmish line. Also, on the march the fife and drum corps kept cadence with tunes such as *The Girl I Left Behind Me*, and *The White Cockade*, and the band played popular tunes in camp like *When Johnny Comes Marching Home* and *Tenting on the Old Camp Ground*.

On occasions, the regimental band played in battle to great effect. At Williamsburg in 1862, III Corps commander Maj Gen Samuel Heintzelman ordered several bands standing-by in the rear to "Play, damn it!" Soon after, the incongruous sound of *Yankee Doodle* and then *Three Cheers for the Red, White, and Blue* rose over the roar of battle (Sears 1992: 75). The music rallied the Union troops and forced the Confederates to withdraw. The survivors of the disastrous Pickett's Charge at Gettysburg on July 3, 1863, returned to their own lines listening to the tune *Nearer, My God, to Thee*. At Five Forks, Union musicians under orders from Maj Gen Philip Sheridan played *Nelly Bly* while under fire in the front line. Gen Robert E. Lee himself said, 'I don't think we could have an army without music' (quoted in Lanning 2006: 243).

A lack of accurate musketry fire was a common problem in battle due to several factors. Many units did not practice musketry with live ammunition on cost grounds, and those that did usually practiced volley fire only, not target shooting, so there was no foolproof way of ensuring that infantrymen were not shooting high before engaging in combat. The close formation of the infantrymen meant that bumping and jostling during reloading often prevented a steady aim. Furthermore, inexperienced troops tended not to allow for the recoil of the musket when firing, which tended to kick the muzzle upwards. Hence, officers often ordered men to aim at the enemy's belt buckles or knees. Although rifle-muskets had leaf or block sights accurately calibrated up to maximum range, it seems that these were seldom adjusted in battle except by a small minority of troops. The customary tactic was to wait until the enemy was within "point blank" range (25yd), which rendered leaf sights unnecessary. Although the first shot was usually fired as a volley by rank, file, or by the whole regiment, only the very best infantry could continue with volley fire on command. Almost without exception "fire at will" took over. While the average infantryman was capable of loading and firing three rounds per minute in a drill situation, it is doubtful whether this was ever achieved for longer than a few minutes in battle. It might take from 40 to 120 minutes to fire off the 40 or 50 rounds carried in the cartridge box. On some occasions it could take much longer.

Normally positioned on the left of the center-right company of a regiment in "line of battle" was the color guard, typically five to 12 NCOs assigned to protect the National and regimental colors, each of which was carried by a color-bearer who held the rank of sergeant. Together, these flags served as an important rallying point for the regiment if its formation loosened or disintegrated in the chaos of battle. Color-bearers were invariably the target of enemy fire, and the honor of carrying flags was given to the strongest men

Skirmishers were provided by the two flank companies of a regiment in both Union and Confederate armies, and were tasked with clearing the way, and protecting the advance, of the main corps. Entitled "Feeling the Enemy," this engraving shows a four-man group of skirmishers. Permitted to carry their weapons "in the manner most convenient to them" two men are ready to fire while the others are loading. Skirmishers often operated hundreds of yards ahead of their main body of troops, and were supported by a small reserve whose duty it was to fill vacant places, furnish the line with cartridges, relieve the fatigued, and serve as a rallying point. Larger bodies of skirmishers, such as a regiment, were supported by a company-sized reserve. (*Battles & Leaders*)

selected from companies throughout the regiment. Every effort was made to replace them if shot down, in order to keep the flag(s) flying, as at Chaffin's Farm/New Market Heights on September 29, 1864.

Within each infantry company, the captain marched on the right of the front rank and the first sergeant in the same position in the rear rank. The remaining officers and sergeants were posted as "file closers" two paces behind the rear rank. Stationed at either end of the file closers were the right and left guides, each of whom held the rank of sergeant. A general marker with the same rank was posted at either end of the regiment, left and right, when in "line of battle." Each of these men carried a small National flag, either on a staff or on a rod stuck in the barrel of his musket, which served as a marker by which the regiment could dress ranks.

Skirmish fire usually preceded a larger fire-fight. A skirmish line was sent out only to make contact with the enemy, not fight him. At regimental level, the two flank companies would be sent forward to fan out and deploy at long-range distance from the enemy. These would be supported by a small reserve which filled vacant places, replenished cartridges, and served as a rallying point. Keeping up a harassing fire, skirmishers would not attempt to attack. In so doing they could feel out enemy strength by probing forward. They could also keep the enemy occupied while a major attack or flanking movement was being assembled. Following combat, the skirmish screen turned into a line of pickets tasked with guarding the perimeters of an encamped army.

Assaults were conducted in several formations, including double-rank "line of battle" with individual regiments side-by-side, assault waves with multiple regiments or brigades in successive waves spaced out loosely one behind the other, and brigade columns with all regiments of a brigade in line one behind the other in close formation. Infantry frequently knelt or laid down to return fire, as at First Bull Run/Manassas. In defensive mode regiments were also drilled to form a "hollow square" of two, and sometimes four, ranks to repel cavalry. Smaller units rallied by battalion, company, or platoon, forming three ranks on all four sides.

First Bull Run/ Manassas

July 21, 1861

BACKGROUND TO BATTLE

In the early days of the Civil War, the aged General-in-Chief, Lt Gen Winfield Scott, proposed a strategy to force the Southern States back into the Union which had two prominent features. First, all ports in the seceding states were to be rigorously blockaded by the Union Navy. Secondly, a strong force of about 80,000 infantrymen should use the Mississippi River as a route to thrust completely through the Confederacy. Scott estimated that manpower and resources for what became known as the "Anaconda Plan" would not be ready until the fall of 1861. His critics called for an immediate overland campaign directed primarily at Richmond, Virginia, established as the Confederate capital on May 30, 1861. Their stated belief was that if a few Southern cities and strongholds were taken, the Confederacy would collapse. Hence, the Union campaign leading to the First Battle of Bull Run/Manassas was very much driven by Northern public opinion. The "Forward to Richmond" campaign was conducted by the *New York Herald*, a Radical Republican newspaper whose editor Horace Greeley did much to pressurize the commander in the field, Brig Gen Irwin McDowell, into advancing on Richmond before his army was ready. As a result, the newly inaugurated President Abraham Lincoln asked the loyal Northern and Border states on April 15, 1861, for 75,000 militiamen for 90 days' service to put down the rebellion. Still influenced by Scott's original strategy, each of the regiments received into Federal service was to be either infantry or riflemen. Thus, the part-time Northern soldiery, supplemented by volunteers with little or no military experience, were expected to defend the Union and bring the Southern slave states to heel within three months.

Commanding the Army of Northeastern Virginia with 30,600 men at his disposal, Brig Gen McDowell was instructed to attack the Confederate forces of Brig Gen P.G.T. Beauregard's Army of the Potomac, amounting to 20,000 men, and drive them from the vital railroad junction at Manassas, Virginia. Meanwhile, Maj Gen Robert Patterson was ordered to advance from Harrisburg, Pennsylvania, with 18,000 men in order to keep the 12,000 Confederate troops under Brig Gen Joseph E. Johnston's Army of the Shenandoah in the Shenandoah Valley and unable to reinforce Beauregard at Manassas.

On July 15, Patterson marched to Bunker Hill, 19 miles into Virginia, and ordered a halt. During the following day, McDowell began his advance toward Manassas but Patterson unfortunately withdrew to Charlestown in order to base his command at Harper's Ferry, thereby taking pressure off Johnston. The bulk of McDowell's troops arrived at Centreville, near Manassas, during the afternoon of July 18. An attack on Beauregard's smaller force on the southern bank of Bull Run within the next 24 hours would probably have achieved a Union victory. But with an inexperienced army, McDowell felt unable to order an immediate assault, although he did launch a "reconnaissance in force" the next day; Brig Gen Daniel Tyler's 1st Division advanced on Brig Gen Milledge L. Bonham's 1st Brigade, Army of the Potomac, at Mitchell's Ford, and Brig Gen James Longstreet's 4th Brigade, Army of the Potomac, at Blackburn's Ford. Tyler was repulsed with a loss of 83 casualties, while the Confederates lost 68 men.

When they learned of McDowell's advance, the Confederate authorities in Richmond immediately ordered Johnston to reinforce Beauregard. Since Patterson had withdrawn the same day, Johnston was able to start immediately via Ashby Gap and thence by rail to Manassas Junction, with his first troops under Brig Gen Thomas J. Jackson arriving during the early hours of July 20. This development is important in military history as one of the first uses of railroad to move troops into battle.

INTO COMBAT

On July 21 McDowell began to execute his battle plan, which involved a 14-mile march to launch an attack on the Confederate left flank. Beauregard had a similar plan to attack the Union right flank, which was nipped in the bud by McDowell. Unfortunately for the Union general, Confederate signallers detected the dust rising from McDowell's flanking movement and flashed the message via signal flags to Col Nathan G. "Shanks" Evans' small 7th Brigade, Army of the Potomac, at the Stone Bridge, "Look out for your left, you are turned." This was one of the earliest uses of signal flags in battle.

Acting on his own initiative, Evans moved all but four companies of his brigade northwest of the Stone Bridge to oppose the enveloping force; Evans' troops were soon joined by the brigades of Brig Gen Barnard E. Bee, Jr. and Col Francis S. Bartow, which had freshly arrived with Johnston from the Shenandoah Valley. Being more familiar with the terrain as he had supervised the construction of field fortifications along the Bull Run line since early June of 1861, Beauregard continued to command the line of battle while his superior Johnston concentrated on passing troops north from Manassas Junction to reinforce Evans.

Initially able to push the Confederates back on to Henry House Hill, the Union infantry lacked cohesion as they were brought into action mostly as separate regiments rather than within their brigade structure. As they marched toward Sudley Ford the divisions of Hunter and Heintzelman, together consisting of about 12,000 troops, were delayed by Tyler's division, which had blocked the road as it advanced toward the Stone Bridge. Under the command of Col Orlando B. Willcox, the 2nd Brigade of Heintzelman's division arrived at Sudley Ford at about 09:30hrs. Willcox's brigade consisted of the 11th New York, 1st Michigan, 38th New York (Scott Life Guard), and the four guns of Capt William A. Arnold's Light Co. D, 2nd U.S. Artillery – the 4th Michigan had been left at Fairfax Station and Fairfax Court House by order of Brig Gen McDowell.

Organized among the firemen of New York City, the 11th New York was raised and initially led by Col Elmer Ellsworth. A former commander of Chicago's famed United States Zouave Cadets, a friend of Abraham Lincoln, and first conspicuous casualty and Northern martyr of the Civil War, Ellsworth, aged only 24, had been shot dead by a secessionist while seizing a Confederate flag during the Federal occupation of Alexandria, Virginia, on May 24, 1861. Hence, the 11th New York were led during the battle by Col Noah L. "Pony" Farnham, despite the fact he was suffering from typhoid fever. Many of the Fire Zouaves had made themselves unpopular among the Southern population by "skirmishing in the countryside o' nights" when Northern troops had occupied the area around Alexandria, Virginia, in May 1861 (*NYEP* June 4, 1861: 2:2). Conspicuous in their red fezzes and red shirts (worn by most of the New York fire companies), they would be the target of revenge for Confederate troops during the forthcoming battle.

According to an exaggerated account from 20-year-old Pvt John Howard Walker of Co. D, the Fire Zouaves attempted to put their Zouave drill into practice as they approached the battlefield and "went twenty miles double quick step and double quick time, and it almost killed us" (*NYH* Jul 27, 1861: 8:3). An enlisted man in Co. E recalled that:

> "double quick," if properly performed, is a very pretty movement, and one not excessively tiresome to the soldier ... But with our regiment, it was another matter, and performed in a manner not set down in our tactics. Anyone who has seen

Assistant Engineer of the New York City Fire Department before the Civil War, Noah Farnham was appointed lieutenant colonel of the 11th New York on May 7, 1861, and led the regiment after Col Elmer Ellsworth was killed during the occupation of Alexandria, Virginia on May 24, 1861. Nicknamed "Pony" because of his small stature, Farnham had his horse shot from under him and was mortally wounded at First Bull Run/ Manassas by a musket ball that deflected off the side of his skull. He wears the field officers' version of the gray first regimental uniform of the Fire Zouaves, and his black arm-band is worn in memory of Col Ellsworth. (Library of Congress LC-B813-1628 C)

MAP KEY

1 08:30hrs: Four companies of Col N.G. Evans' small 7th Brigade of the Confederate Army of the Potomac take up positions northwest of the Stone Bridge to oppose the enveloping force, after Confederate signal officer Capt E. Porter Alexander spies the Union flanking movement. At about 10:50hrs Evans is joined by the Army of the Shenandoah's 3rd Brigade (Bee) and 2nd Brigade (Bartow), both of which have arrived with Brig Gen Joseph E. Johnston from the Shenandoah Valley.

2 09:30hrs: After a 14-mile march commencing at 02:30hrs, the 2nd Division (Hunter) and the 11th New York's parent division, the Third Division (Heintzelman), both of the Union Army of Northeastern Virginia, arrive at Sudley Ford. En route they had been delayed by Union Brig Gen Tyler's First Division, which had blocked the road as it advanced toward the Stone Bridge over Bull Run.

3 09:45hrs (approx.): The men of the 11th New York discard their overcoats and haversacks at Sudley Church and then, forming in "column of companies," advance along the Manassas Road behind the 38th New York.

4 11:00hrs: Confederate forces under Evans, Bee, and Bartow fall back and take up new positions on Henry House Hill after a fierce half-hour fire-fight against elements of Hunter's Second Division.

5 11:30hrs (approx.): Sherman's 1st Brigade and Keyes' 3rd Brigade, both of Tyler's First Division, cross Bull Run, just north of the Stone Bridge.

6 11:35hrs (approx.): Heintzelman's Third Division arrives near the junction of the Warrenton and Manassas roads, and Willcox's 2nd Brigade is deployed in "line of battle" with the 11th New York to the right and 38th New York to the left of Capt Arnold's Co. D, 2nd U.S. Artillery, deploying four guns. The 11th New York is ordered to lie down to shelter from the heavy musketry fire.

7 12:00hrs (approx.): Jackson's 1st Brigade, Army of the Shenandoah – including the 33rd Virginia – arrives having marched about 7 miles at "quick time" from near Blackburn's and Mitchell's fords on Bull Run and a new Confederate line of battle is formed on the southeast slope of Henry House Hill, about 400yd from the Henry House.

8 13:30hrs (approx.): The 11th New York and the 14th Brooklyn are ordered forward to support the batteries of Griffin (Co. D, 5th U.S. Artillery) and Ricketts (Co. I, 1st U.S. Artillery) south of the Manassas Road/Warrenton Turnpike crossroads.

9 14:30hrs (approx.): With the 1st Minnesota on the right, the 11th New York advances up Henry House Hill in "line of battle" toward the concealed left wing of the reinforced Confederate line.

10 15:00hrs (approx.): Disobeying Jackson's order to wait until the enemy is within 30yd, the 33rd Virginia opens fire and charges.

11 15:05hrs (approx.): The 11th New York is thrown back and Rickett's battery is captured as the Union gunners mistake some of the blue-coated 33rd Virginia for friendly troops.

12 15:15hrs (approx.): Remnants of the 11th New York rally farther down the hillside and with elements of Hunter's Second Division counterattack, throwing the 33rd Virginia back and helping to re-take the abandoned guns of Rickett's battery, which the New Yorkers fail to use.

13 15:25hrs (approx.): Elements of the 1st Virginia Volunteer Cavalry debouch from the woods to the south and charge at the right flank of the 11th New York. The remnants of the 11th New York rally and once again advance up Henry House Hill with elements of the 1st Minnesota, 38th New York, and 14th Brooklyn.

14 15.30hrs: Jackson orders the rest of his brigade to open fire and charge with fixed bayonets. The guns of Rickett's battery change hands several more times. Other Confederate units join in the general advance, and Union regiments including the 11th New York recoil and fall back.

15 16:00hrs (approx.): The Union retreat becomes a full-scale rout as the exhausted and battle-weary Union troops rush back across Sudley Ford and the Stone Bridge, and beyond to Washington, D.C.

Battlefield environment

The terrain north of Manassas, Virginia, consisted of patchy woodland mainly composed of pine and virgin oak with open fields along the turnpikes, or toll roads. Much of the countryside north of the Warrenton Pike through which the Union flanking attack advanced from Sudley Ford was thickly wooded, but the land around Stone Bridge was well cleared except for the steeper bluffs and consisted of large rolling fields. A river, named Bull Run, dissected the area from its source 15 miles away in the Bull Run Mountains, and was about 13yd wide at its widest point. A tributary called Young's Branch flowed from west to east where most of the fighting took place.

Entrenched alongside masked batteries or concealed behind makeshift breastworks, Confederate infantrymen guarded crossing points and fords from Stone Bridge to Union Mills. Heavy rainstorms earlier in the month had deepened the Run, making crossing at the fords difficult. Most accounts state that the weather was hot and humid on the day of the battle.

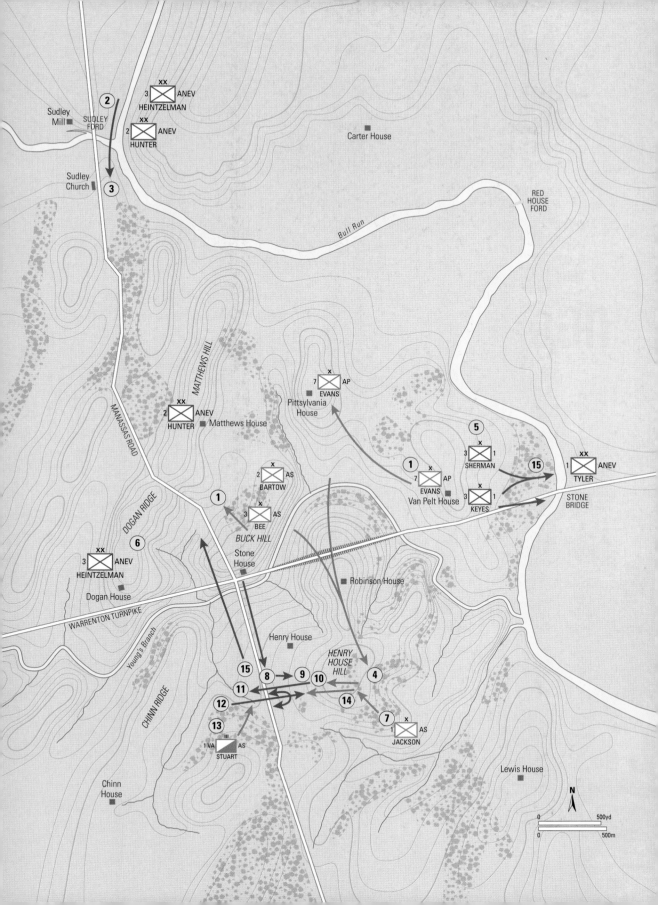

Sudley Mill

SUDLEY FORD

2 ☒ ANEV
3 HEINTZELMAN

2 ☒ ANEV
2 HUNTER

Sudley Church

3

Carter House

RED HOUSE FORD

Bull Run

MATTHEWS HILL

2 ☒ ANEV
2 HUNTER
Matthews House

Pittsylvania House

7 ☒ AP
EVANS

5

3 ☒ 1
SHERMAN

15 ☒ ANEV
1 TYLER

MANASSAS ROAD

2 ☒ AS
BARTOW

1

3 ☒ AS
BEE

BUCK HILL

Stone House

1 ☒ AP
7 EVANS
Van Pelt House

3 ☒ 1
KEYES

STONE BRIDGE

DOGAN RIDGE

6

3 ☒ ANEV
3 HEINTZELMAN

Dogan House

Robinson House

WARRENTON TURNPIKE

Young's Branch

Henry House

HENRY HOUSE HILL

4

CHINN RIDGE

15

8 **9** **10**

11

12

14

7 ☒ AS
JACKSON

13

1 VA ☷ AS
STUART

Chinn House

Lewis House

N

0   500yd
0   500m

a closely contested race between two fire engine companies down Grand Street can form a good idea of what double quick was with us. ("Tiger! Zouave!!" website)

An enlisted man in Co. A, 2nd Maine Volunteer Infantry, did observe "the red-shirted and red-capped Zouaves" rush past "at the double quick" during the Union advance toward Manassas Junction (*LDEJ* Jul 30, 1861: 2:1).1/Lt Edward B. Knox described how the 11th New York

Published in the *Illustrated London News* on June 22, 1861, this engraving depicts the 11th New York turning out at the "quick step" to support pickets while encamped between Alexandria and Fairfax Court House, Virginia. (Author's collection)

moved briskly forward through the woods, singing and laughing and eager for the fight. They had marched about fourteen miles, and were within three miles of the battle-field, when they heard the guns and saw the smoke from an eminence. This excited the men wonderfully, and at a double-quick step they pressed on, with the intention of joining [brigade commander] Col. Wilcox [*sic*], who, with the [1st] Michigan regiment, was a short way ahead. Halting at a pool of dirty water, they refreshed themselves, and went on until they came to a church … where they left their overcoats and haversacks [plus blanket rolls and canteens if empty], and having formed by companies, again went on at double-quick step. (*NYT* Jul 26, 1861: 2:2)

Willcox's troops joined the other brigades of Heintzelman's division, plus those of Tyler's and Hunter's divisions, on Dogan's Ridge and Matthew's Hill, and waited for orders from McDowell. At about 11:30hrs a courier finally arrived from Heintzelman ordering Willcox to proceed toward the noise of battle. According to an unidentified Fire Zouave, "After we'd been a standing three hours … in the grass, up come a long-legged cuss, and says he, follow me" (*TGE* Sep 1, 1861: 3:3). Willcox's brigade advanced at the double-quick with the 38th New York in front and 11th New York, consisting of 942 men, bringing up the rear. Arriving near the junction of the Warrenton and Manassas roads, the two regiments were deployed into "line of battle" with the 11th New York to the right and 38th New York to the left of the four guns of Arnold's battery. Several minutes later the Zouaves were ordered to lie down in a stubble field "under cover of a fence" to shelter themselves from the "heavy fire of musketry" flying overhead from the Confederate infantry concealed in the woods to their front.

The Union infantrymen wearing fezzes in this cracked glass ambrotype are believed to have belonged to the 11th New York. They wear what replaced their "shoddy" first uniform. (Library of Congress LC-B8184-10696)

Willcox next received an order to send a regiment to support Capt J.B. Ricketts' Light Co. I,

1st U.S. Artillery, and Capt C. Griffin's Light Co. D, 5th U.S. Artillery, both of which had been ordered to take up a position farther south along the Manassas Road, about 300yd from the enemy. Although they would be able to deliver an enfilade fire, these batteries would now be perilously close to the Confederate lines. Recognizing his guns were being placed in a poor position, Griffin doubted that the inexperienced 11th New York would be able to protect his guns, saying, "I will go, but mark my words, they will not support us" (quoted in Patterson 1865: 99). Maj William

Barry, McDowell's Chief of Artillery, rode over to the Fire Zouaves to personally lead them to their position to the right of the 11 guns.

Up to this point the Confederates under Evans, Bee, and Bartow had fallen back as a result of the initial impact of the Union advance. They now rallied around Brig Gen Thomas J. Jackson's 1st Brigade, Army of the Shenandoah, consisting of five Virginian volunteer infantry regiments including the 33rd Virginia plus Lt John P. Brockenbrough's Rockbridge (Virginia) Artillery, which arrived at about 12:00hrs having completed a seven-mile march from behind Blackburn's and Mitchell's fords on Bull Run on the right of the Confederate line. They now rallied around the brigade of Brig Gen Thomas J. Jackson, which formed a new battle line on the southeast slope of a ridgeline about 400yd from the Henry House, which Bee called a "stonewall," thus earning the Virginian general the sobriquet "Stonewall" Jackson. The Confederate force awaiting Willcox's troops now consisted of about 6,500 infantry, 13 pieces of artillery, and several companies of Col J.E.B. Stuart's 1st Virginia Volunteer Cavalry.

As the men of the 11th New York advanced in support of Ricketts' battery in "line of battle" with an eight-company front and the flank companies, A and H, in reserve, they were joined on their right by the 1st Minnesota (1st Brigade, Third Division). As the two Union infantry regiments advanced in close formation, both Ricketts' and Griffin's batteries were unlimbering and placing their guns. Pvt Walker of Co. D, 11th New York, recalled, "We had a hard fight. The bullets flew like hailstones around me, and I had to dodge cannon balls" (*NYH* Jul 27, 1861: 8:3). Another unidentified Zouave stated that the Fire Zouaves went forward "first short, and then double-quick. All of a sudden pop, bang, bang, bang went the bloody guns on our left, that God only knew was there, for we didn't, and the boys fell down like sheep" (*TGE* Sep 1, 1861: 3:3). In his rather succinct after-battle report, Willcox stated: "The ground was slightly rising before us, and the enemy opened a heavy but not destructive fire as we reached the crest" (Scott 1880–1901, I, 2: 408).

LEFT
Pvt Peter Lauck Kurtz, Marion Rifles (Co. A), 5th Virginia, arrived on Henry House Hill with Jackson's brigade at about 12:00hrs on July 21, 1861, and soon after was involved in the charge that turned the tide of battle at First Bull Run/Manassas. (Library of Congress LC-DIG-ppmsca-32596)

RIGHT
Also involved in the fateful charge at First Bull Run/ Manassas, Pvt James M. Trussell, Letcher Riflemen (Co. H), 2nd Virginia, was wounded, sustaining a broken leg. (Author's collection)

William Noll, 11th New York

Typical of the volunteers of 1861, 19-year-old William Noll was of German origin and had migrated to the United States aboard the steamer *Bremen* in August of 1859. Working as a baker in Brooklyn, New York City, he enlisted in Co. D, 11th New York, on April 20, 1861. Following about two weeks of drilling and camp life, Noll witnessed the death of his commanding officer, Col Elmer Ellsworth, on May 24, 1861, as Ellsworth removed a Confederate flag from the Marshall House during the occupation of Alexandria, Virginia.

On July 21, 1861, Noll was probably filled with as much optimism, plus a need to revenge the death of his commanding officer, as his red-shirted comrades as they advanced up Henry House Hill at First Bull Run/ Manassas. Unfortunately, the day ended as badly for Noll, as it did for the 11th New York, and indeed the whole Army of Northeastern Virginia as it was routed and fled back to Washington, D.C. He was shot through the left foot, captured and held as a prisoner of war from July 23, 1861, following which he had some of the bone in his foot removed by a Confederate surgeon. Upon his release and exchange at Newport News, Virginia, he was assessed as unfit for further military duty and discharged on March 12, 1862.

Pvt William Noll served in the 11th New York until wounded and captured at First Bull Run/Manassas on July 21, 1861. He wears the regimental gray uniform, which was worn out and replaced before the battle. (Richard Ricca collection)

The two Union infantry regiments were soon to find themselves confronting the 33rd Virginia, on the left wing of Jackson's line.

The 33rd Virginia consisted of some of the finest militia units in the Shenandoah Valley and was commanded by Col Arthur C. Cummings, a prominent lawyer from Abingdon, Virginia, and a graduate of the Virginia Military Institute who had served in the Mexican–American War. The eight companies of his under-strength regiment, amounting to 560 officers and men, had received a "cold bite" at dawn before marching at the "double-quick" with the rest of Jackson's brigade. They took up position at the extreme left end of the Confederate line. Here the men of the 33rd Virginia lay prostrate for about two hours, just behind the crest of the hill and out of sight of the enemy, with the 2nd Virginia to their right, the 4th and 27th Virginia in support of the four guns of Capt W.N. Pendleton's 1st Rockbridge Artillery, and the 5th Virginia forming the right wing of Jackson's brigade. In his diary, 2/Lt John Grabill of the Tenth Legion Minute Men (Co. C), 33rd Virginia, wrote:

> After marching and counter marching for sometime [*sic*] we were stationed within a-half mile of the battle ground. The regular roaring of the cannon, enlivened by volleys of musketry and the shouts of our boys, whenever they charged produced a combination of sounds as rare as grand. We were then marched to a position on the left of Capt. Pendleton's battery … where we were

John O. Casler, 33rd Virginia

Also of German origin, 22-year-old John Overton Casler enlisted in the Potomac Guards, one of the first infantry companies recruited in Hampshire County, Virginia, for one year on June 6, 1861. Casler's great-grandfather, Michael Kessler, migrated to America prior to the outbreak of the Revolutionary War. After settling on a farm near Frederick, Maryland, he changed the family name to a more American version. On the death of Michael Casler, his son John then moved to Virginia. By 1811 his son, also named Michael Casler, lived in Springfield, Hampshire County, where he married and engaged in the dual occupation of farmer and shoemaker. The first of four children, John O. Casler was born in 1838 and, at 20 years of age, went west to seek his fortune. Getting only as far as Missouri, he tried his hand at farming and stock-raising, but when the Civil War began in 1861 he rushed back to Virginia to enlist, following which he fought bravely within the ranks of the 33rd Virginia at First Bull Run/Manassas, and went on to serve throughout the rest of the war.

John O. Casler produced this self-portrait in 1863 by which time he was a veteran of the "Stonewall Brigade." (*John O. Casler's Four Years in the Stonewall Brigade*)

ordered to lie down. We remained for more than an hour, exposed to a heavy fire. (*SH* Jan 8, 1909: 1)

Of the time spent in this position, Pvt John O. Casler of the Potomac Guards (Co. A) recalled that, "we were shaking hands and bidding farewell to those we were acquainted with, knowing that in a few moments many of us would be stretched lifeless in the field" (Casler 1906: 25). According to Sgt Harrison B. Jones of the Page Greys (Co. H), "we were drawn up in line a battle [*sic*] … one of our company was wounded in the leg … we remained in that position some time exposed to heavy fire from the Federal forces" (Bull Runnings website).

As the Union infantry approached the left wing of his brigade, Jackson sent a staff officer to Col Cummings ordering him to wait until the attackers were within 30yd and then fire, following which Cummings' men were to fix bayonets and charge. Hearing this order, 44-year-old Pvt Thomas McGraw of the Potomac Guards (Co. A), turned to Casler and declared, "That's closer quarters than I anticipated" (quoted in Reidenbaugh 1987: 8). Observing the Union troops advancing toward his position, Cummings informed his men, "They are coming, now wait until they get close before you shoot" (quoted in Casler 1906: 42). However, seeing some men in his regiment being panicked when a solid shot landed close to them, he decided to disobey Jackson's instruction, and hastily ordered his regiment to open fire and charge while the Union infantrymen were still about 70yd distant. He later justified his action by stating that "the most trying position that raw men, and even the best disciplined and bravest could be placed in, was to be required to remain still, doing nothing and receiving the enemy's fire without returning it" (quoted in Reidenbaugh 1987: 8).

Not all of Cummings' men were aware of the change of orders, however. Recalling the moment the front rank of the 11th New York came into view over the crest of the slope, Sgt Maj Randolph Barton stated that, "several of our men rose from the ranks, levelled their muskets at the line, and, although I called out, 'Do not fire yet,' it was no use; they fired" (quoted in Casler 1906: 42). Further confusion occurred when Cummings mistook approaching enemy infantry for friends and ordered those who could hear him to cease fire. Quickly realizing his mistake and anxious to silence Ricketts' battery, he bellowed, "Attention! Forward march! Charge bayonets! Double quick!" According to Barton, "away the regiment went, firing as they ran, into the ranks of the enemy, and particularly at the battery toward which our line rapidly approached" (quoted in Casler 1906: 42). Sgt Jones of the Page Greys (Co. H) recalled, "We then fired a round or two and charged upon the enemy running them from their cannon … our company lost 6 killed & fifteen wounded besides several others marked a little" (Bull Runnings website). Grabill recorded, "After a partial fire we charged them and drove them from their battery of rifled cannon … Our company [the Tenth Legion Minute Men] fought bravely and lost severely" (*SH* Jan 8, 1909). In a letter written to his parents three days after the battle, Casler stated more fully that the 11th New York "did not see us, as we were under the brow of the hill, and they were ordered to fire, but we were too soon for them. We fired first, and advanced, and then they fired. We then charged bayonets, yelling like savages, and they retreated, and our regiment took their artillery …" (Casler 1906: 38). In fact, as the right wing of the 11th New York was thrown back, the gunners of Ricketts' battery momentarily mistook some of the blue-coated infantry of the 33rd Virginia for Union troops and were overrun before they could rectify matters.

The Fire Zouaves attempted to rally farther down the hillside, determined to win back the abandoned guns. According to 1/Lt Knox they became

> impressed with the idea … to retake those guns. Whereupon with a wild, wild yell, three cheers and a loud, fierce cry of "Remember Ellsworth," they dashed across the intervening space, rushed in the face of a murderous discharge from the cannon on the hill, and with loud whoops and hurrahs drove some away, killed the rest, and occupied the position. (*NYT* Jul 26, 1861: 2:2)

An unidentified Zouave recalled several days after the battle:

> And then the way we took them batteries. Well, you ought to have seen it – that's all. We saw our men drove away from their guns, and we made up our minds to get 'em, and we charged, yelling like bloody hell, drove the seceshes [secessionists or Confederates] back a deuced sight quicker than they come, and popped 'em down at every shot. But when we'd got the guns the fellers didn't come to hold 'em, and of course we couldn't work 'em, and we left. (*NYT* Jul 26, 1861: 2:2)

On the receiving end of this counterattack, 2/Lt Grabill later wrote, "After holding the field for sometime [*sic*], our number becoming less every moment, we left the battery expecting to rally our men for another charge. So many were killed, wounded and scattered that an attempt to rally proved ineffectual" (*SH* Jan 8, 1909). Stunned, the remnants of the 33rd Virginia recoiled back up the hill and collapsed against the 2nd Virginia, causing additional confusion.

In the mean time, elements of three companies of Stuart's 1st Virginia Cavalry, erroneously called the "Black Horse Cavalry" by Union forces, charged "full upon" the Fire Zouaves from woods on their right. Knox recalled that the Fire Zouaves

Entitled "Charge of the Black Horse Cavalry upon the Fire Zouaves at Bull Run," this fanciful engraving was published in *Harper's Weekly* on August 10, 1861, and illustrates the chaos of battle at First Bull Run/Manassas. The bare-chested men are in indication of the heat in which the battle was fought. (Author's collection)

formed hastily in line, kneeling, semi-kneeling and standing, that, Ellsworth fashion, they might receive their enemies with successive volleys. On came the horse – a full regiment of brave men, splendidly mounted, and as ready for mischief as those on whom they hoped to fall. To an early discharge from the cavalry the Zouaves made no response, although several of the men were killed, but waited patiently until the enemy was almost upon them, when in quick succession, the three ranks fired, each man doing his best for the good cause. (*NYT* Jul 26, 1861: 2:2)

"Remember Ellsworth!"

Seen through the eyes of an enlisted man of the 11th New York, the 33rd Virginia are depicted here at the moment they launched their charge down Henry House Hill, "yelling like savages," during the battle of First Bull Run/Manassas on July 21, 1861. In what was considered a major turning point in the battle, the Fire Zouaves were sent reeling back down the hill, abandoning the guns of Rickett's battery, which were captured by the Confederates. Col Arthur C. Cummings is seen urging his regiment on in the background. A dismounted field officer wearing the gray first uniform received by the 11th New York in May 1861, and armed with sword and Colt Army revolver, orders the Fire Zouaves to stand their ground as the two regiments clash. Some of the Virginians wear dark-blue uniforms as prescribed for the Virginia State Militia in 1858, while others have gray coats or hunting shirts with trim of various colors. The lack of uniformity in both armies resulted in regiments mistaking friend for foe, and vice versa, during the battle.

Determined to avenge the death of their beloved commander, Col Elmer Ellsworth, who was shot dead while taking down a secession flag during the occupation of Alexandria, Virginia, on May 24, 1861, the Fire Zouaves used the battle cry "Remember Ellsworth!" as they braced themselves to meet the enemy. Their red caps and firemen's shirts made them very conspicuous during the fighting. Some wear white cotton Havelock cap covers, which proved unpopular as the war unfolded. The men of the 33rd Virginia carry a mixture of Model 1842 percussion and Model 1816 flintlock muskets at "Charge – bayonet." The line companies of the 11th New York are loading and firing Model 1855 rifle-muskets while the two flank companies (not shown) were armed with the Model 1855 rifle with sword bayonet.

Flags served as rallying points for both armies throughout the Civil War. A First National flag bearing 11 stars in its canton is carried by the 33rd Virginia. The 11th New York wave a National flag and a regimental flag presented by the New York City Fire Department bearing a trophy of firemen's equipment including helmet, trumpet, axe, hook, and ladder.

Not part of Ellsworth's drill manual, but included in that part of Hardee's *Tactics* entitled "Instruction for Skirmishers," this maneuver was indeed designed to repel cavalry and was known as "Rally by platoon." Adding further detail, an unidentified Fire Zouave commented:

> Well, Sir, they came a riding down on to us like the very devil, and we just come the three-rank arrangement on 'em – one rank was down there, the second just above their shoulders, and the third fellers stood up straight. On they came – sword and pistol in hand, and the horses galloping like damnation. Don't fire till they get way up, says Pony [Col Farnham] – and we didn't. The cusses didn't know what to make of it but we soon informed 'em. Pop went the first rank, and the poor devils fell out of their saddles like dead sheep. Bang went number two, and down come another batch, and I'll be damned if I believe there was a third of 'em left when they turned tail and scud away, as if all hell was after 'em. (*NYT* Jul 26, 1861: 2:2)

Knox concluded, "Not more than a hundred of them rode off, and as they went their rebellious ears were saluted with [a popular rallying cry among American Zouave units] 'One, two, three, four, five, six, seven, eight, tiger, Zouave,' and such a 'tiger repeat' as one can only appreciate when he has heard it."

Soon after this, any regimental cohesion within the 11th New York disappeared. Farnham had been wounded in the head but managed to remain at his post, supported by Lt Col Cregier and Maj Leoser. Sustaining five killed, one wounded, and six captured, with Capt John Downey among the latter, Co. D had disintegrated. Within Co. G, Ensign Daniel Divver was killed and 1/Lt Andrew Underhill was captured along with three enlisted men.

Losing one man killed and five captured, Co. C became particularly disorganized; overcome with exhaustion earlier in the action, Capt Michael C. Murphy had been carried "off the field", while 1/Lt Louis Fitzgerald was also incapacitated by a wound during the clash with the Confederate horsemen, and was "led off the field" immediately afterward. Ensign John A. Smith was "struck in the forehead and knocked insensible" and carried to the rear, following which, according to Cpl John Kerrigan, the remainder of Co. C "fell in as best they could with the other companies of the regiment" (*NYH* Jul 30, 1861: 2:4).

Nevertheless, remnants of the 11th New York, joined by the 14th Brooklyn, 1st Minnesota, and 38th New York, once again started up the hill. Observing the renewed advance of the enemy, Jackson ordered forward the other regiments of his brigade. Leaping from their concealment below the brow of the hill, they delivered a deadly fusillade and the Union line dissolved. An action initiated by the premature charge of the 33rd Virginia contrary to orders had finally thrown the exhausted and battle-weary Union troops into complete chaos and confusion. Sgt Maj Barton, 33rd Virginia, concluded, "The suddenness of our attack, the boldness of it, for our men went over and past the battery, the disabling of the guns, all checked the advancing line" (quoted in Casler 1906: 43).

Of his futile efforts to check the faltering Fire Zouaves, Knox recalled:

What happened after that, it is hard to detail. Grape and cannister [*sic*] were poured in upon them thick and fast. Down on their faces till the shot passed on

Produced in the 1880s by artist Isaac Walton Taber, this illustration depicts elements of the 11th New York, 1st Minnesota, and 14th Brooklyn advancing up Henry House Hill in an effort to retake the guns of Ricketts' battery. (*Battles & Leaders*)

fell every man, and then "up and at em" till the next volley, was the cry of them all. This continued for a long time, during which squad after squad was used up, man after man fell dead, or receiving a shot while on the ground, failed to rise at the next command. Then came the order to retreat, which slowly and gradually was obeyed. The regiment broke ranks – some of the men walked slowly off; others went into the woods and fought from behind the trees on their own hook; others falling in with different regiments, joined forces against the common enemy, and others climbed the trees to see "what was up." While in the woods the slaughter amongst the men was very great, and the cross fire to which they were there exposed did them more damage than all else beside. The retreat with them was as with all the regiments – not particularly an orderly one, but rather a free and easy retrograde movement, which, if not a stampede or a rout, was at least a very unmilitary operation. (*NYT* Jul 26, 1861: 2:2)

Despite reports in the Southern press that it was "almost annihilated," the 11th New York received a lesser number of casualties than the 33rd Virginia. The latter paid dearly during their charge on Henry House Hill, sustaining 37 killed and 98 wounded, and eight missing in action, whereas the 11th New York had 27 killed, 23 wounded, and 56 captured.

Entitled "Rallying the troops of Bee, Bartow, and Evans, behind the Robinson House," this engraving by J.W. Evans depicts Brig Gen Thomas J. Jackson forming his brigade on Henry House Hill in order to launch a Confederate counterattack at First Bull Run/Manassas. (*Battles & Leaders*)

"The Bloody Angle," Gettysburg

July 3, 1863

BACKGROUND TO BATTLE

The Confederate victory at First Bull Run/Manassas had two main effects. First, it caused great celebration throughout the South. Secondly, it strengthened the demand for an immediate forward movement to capture the Northern capital. Despite great public pressure to act, the Confederate Army remained stationary and went into winter quarters around Fairfax Court House in northern Virginia. This soon led to bitter disputes and recriminations, and the president was accused of preventing the Confederate Army from following up its victory. The generals wanted to concentrate much of the Confederate Army at Richmond for an invasion of the North, but Davis refused to take their advice. The inactive camp life during the winter of 1861/62, with its disease and homesickness, began to make the first important inroads on the war enthusiasm of the Confederate infantryman.

When Davis finally countenanced offensive operations, Robert E. Lee commanded the Army of Northern Virginia. Under Lee the Confederate Army was to make two important attempts to invade the North – the Antietam/Sharpsburg Campaign of 1862 and the Gettysburg Campaign of 1863. By July of 1863, McClellan's Peninsula Campaign had failed to capture Richmond, Second Bull Run/Manassas and Fredericksburg had been lost by Union commanders Pope and Burnside respectively, and Hooker had been routed at Chancellorsville. The only success for the Union Army was at Antietam, Maryland, where, on September 17, 1862, Lee was stopped in his tracks by McClellan.

Confederate forces in Virginia went on the offensive and invaded the North for a second time on June 3, 1863, with the intention of capturing

Photographed in 1861 having recently enlisted in the Charlotte Greys (Co. I), 56th Virginia, Pvt John T. Dixon holds a D-handle Bowie knife and has a Model 1849 Pocket Colt revolver tucked into his belt. (Courtesy of John D. Whitfield)

Washington, D.C., and thus forcing the Union to accept co-existence with the Confederacy. Marching an army of 75,054 men into Pennsylvania, Lee stumbled across the 83,289-strong Union Army of the Potomac under the recently appointed Maj Gen George G. Meade at Gettysburg on July 1 while looking for shoes for his footsore soldiers. The Union defenders were driven back through the streets of Gettysburg to Cemetery Hill, and during the night reinforcements were received by both armies. On July 2, Lee attempted to envelop the Union Army on Cemetery Ridge, first striking its left flank at the Peach Orchard, Wheatfield, Devil's Den, and the Round Tops with Longstreet's and Hill's divisions. He then attacked the Union right at Culp's Hill and East Cemetery Hill with Ewell's divisions. By evening, Meade retained Little Round Top and had repulsed most of Ewell's men. During the morning of July 3, the Confederate infantry were driven from their last toehold on Culp's Hill. Later that afternoon, Lee gambled on success with an infantry attack in grand Napoleonic style on the Union center on Cemetery Ridge, which was preceded by a mass artillery bombardment involving 164 guns.

INTO COMBAT

Popularly called "Pickett's charge" but more accurately known as Pickett's/Pettigrew's/Trimble's charge, Lee's grand assault was planned for three Confederate divisions, commanded by Maj Gen George Pickett, Brig Gen J. Johnston Pettigrew, and Maj Gen Isaac R. Trimble. Approximately 12,000 men in nine infantry brigades were ordered to advance over open fields for three-fourths of a mile (1,320yd) under heavy Union artillery and musketry fire toward a copse of trees on Cemetery Ridge. In addition, two brigades from Maj Gen Richard H. Anderson's Division of Hill's Third Corps, under Brig Gen Cadmus M. Wilcox and Col David Lang (Perry's Brigade), were to support the Confederate attack on the right flank.

George Washington Beidelman wears a regulation infantry overcoat, a substantial garment with short cape and stand-up collar made of sky-blue woolen kersey, under which is the blue uniform issued to the 71st Pennsylvania late in 1861. Officers were also ordered to wear overcoats about the same time to make them less conspicuous on the battlefield. (USAMHI – RG98S-CWP 5.49, Katherine Vanderslice Collection)

At dawn (about 05:50hrs) Pickett's Division was deployed on the right of the Confederate line behind woodland on the eastern side of Seminary Ridge. As they were south of the copse of trees on Cemetery Ridge, these troops would need to adjust the progress of their advance by conducting a difficult "left oblique" maneuver in order to link up with the divisions of Pettigrew and Trimble. Among them was the 56th Virginia Volunteer Infantry, which was part of Garnett's Brigade. Composed of men from the central counties of Virginia and commanded by VMI graduate Col William D. Stuart, the 56th Virginia had fought in Tennessee where it was captured and, following exchange, returned to its home state. Having sustained about 100 casualties during the Seven Days' Battles, this regiment carried only 40 men into action at Antietam/Sharpsburg in September of 1862, but by July 3, 1863, conscription and re-enlistment, plus new volunteers, had boosted its ranks to 289 men.

Commanding the Mecklenburg Guards (Co. A), 56th Virginia, 1/Lt Frank W. Nelson recalled, "Our brigade reached Gettysburg at twilight of the 2d, and orders were issued for us to cook three days' rations. It did not take this to tell us that a great battle impended. We had breakfast before daylight on the 3d and by dawn were in line, ready for whatever came" (*TD* Sep 28, 1936). While awaiting further orders, 1/Lt George Finley of the Harrison Guards (Co. K), 56th Virginia, observed that "Generals Lee, Longstreet, Pickett, and others remained dismounted in our rear for a good while. Staff officers were coming and going, but no orders were issued to us" (*BEN* May 29, 1894). At about 12:00hrs, the Confederate infantry was moved forward through the woods and ordered to lay down immediately behind the artillery. 1/Lt Finley's company was placed so close to the guns of Maj James Dearing's 38th Virginia Light Artillery Battalion that the infantry had to "break to the rear" in order to give "the men at the limber chest room to handle the ammunition" (*BEN* May 29, 1894).

The Confederate artillery began to pound the Union lines at 13:07hrs. While the solid shot wreaked havoc among the Union troops on Cemetery Ridge for the next two hours, explosive rounds such as case and shell were ineffectual due to the inaccurate rate of burn of the fuses contained therein. Hence, much of the Union infantry and artillery on the opposite ridge remained intact. Meanwhile, the Confederate infantry suffered greatly from the Union counter-bombardment and intense heat of the day. According to 1/Lt Finley, "We could see nothing whatever of the opposing lines, but knew from the firing that they must have a strong position and many guns" (*BEN* May 29, 1894). Just before the bombardment ceased, Longstreet, who doubted that the attack would succeed, rode slowly from right to left between his bellowing artillery and prostrate infantry, inspecting the lines of his corps.

At about 15:00hrs the great bombardment ended. Soon the command "Fall in!" was issued by brigade commanders and those nearby heard Pickett shout as he rode out in front of his division, "Up men, and to your posts! Don't forget that you are from old Virginia!" (quoted in Tsouras 1992: 165). Within each infantry company, the captain, or senior officer, occupied the right end of the front rank, while the lieutenants and sergeants served as file closers behind the second rank. The average strength of a company in Pickett's Division on July 3, 1863, was 29 all ranks, including three officers. Many companies had been weakened by details for skirmishers. According to 1/Lt Nelson of Co. A, Col Stuart ordered the file closers of his regiment to see that "all the men kept up, and if any lagged shoot them, or he would have the file-closers themselves shot" (*TD* Sep 28, 1936).1/Lt Finley of Co. K recalled:

In this print, based on a painting by Henry Alexander Ogden, George Pickett receives orders from Longstreet prior to the Confederate assault on Cemetery Ridge at Gettysburg on July 3, 1863. The field glasses carried by the latter would have given him a good view of the Union lines on Cemetery Ridge. (Library of Congress LC-USZ62-43635)

MAP KEY

1 05:00hrs (approx.): Pickett's Division is deployed on the right of the Confederate line behind woodland on the eastern side of Seminary Ridge.

2 12:00hrs (approx.): the Confederate infantry is moved forward through Spangler's Wood and ordered to lay down immediately behind the artillery of Maj James Dearing's 38th Virginia Light Artillery Battalion.

3 15:00hrs: the Confederate artillery falls silent after nearly two hours of cannonading; the 15 infantry regiments of Pickett's Division are ordered to stand up and at 15:10hrs advance toward Cemetery Ridge. Within a few minutes the order "left oblique" is given and the whole division turns about 45 degrees to the left, and begins to close in on Pettigrew's division. The Union artillery of McGilvery's reserve artillery line opens an enfilading fire and begins to devastate the Confederate infantry of Pickett's Division.

4 15:00hrs (approx.): Col R. Penn Smith, commanding the 71st Pennsylvania, orders his two exposed companies to load extra rifle-muskets and retire behind the stone wall about 65yd to their rear.

5 15:20hrs (approx.): Disappearing from the enemy's view in the first swale which shelters them from most of the Union fire, the infantrymen of Garnett's Brigade halt for several minutes to dress ranks.

6 15:25hrs: Having resumed its advance, Garnett's Brigade climbs over the "crossed-post" fence and proceeds on, with Armistead's Brigade and Kemper's Brigade following.

7 15:33hrs (approx.): Garnett's Brigade reaches the "post-and-rail" fence at the Emmitsburg Road and the Union artillery opens fire with canister. The remainder of the brigade, followed by those of Armistead and Kemper, charges "The Bloody Angle."

8 15:36hrs (approx.): Some men of the 71st Pennsylvania break ranks and withdraw to the rear, while remnants of the 56th Virginia fight their way over the stone-wall fence, achieving what becomes known as "the High Tide of the Confederacy."

9 15:40hrs (approx.): The remnants of the 71st Pennsylvania rally and Union reinforcements counterattack, driving the Confederates back over the stone-wall fence. The defeated Confederates retreat back to their lines on Seminary Ridge; Lee withdraws from Gettysburg the next day.

Battlefield environment

The events surrounding the Confederate grand assault at Gettysburg on July 3, 1863, began on Seminary Ridge, which runs north and south, about three-quarters of a mile west of the town. This ridge was named for the Lutheran Theological Seminary located thereon between the Chambersburg Pike and the Hagerstown Road. The target for the assault was Cemetery Ridge, which is a low swell or roll of land south of Gettysburg stretching a distance of about 2 miles and terminating in two bold, steep hills called Little Round Top and Big Round Top. In 1863 Cemetery Ridge was generally open, except for some woods where it decreases in elevation just north of Little Round Top, and Ziegler's Grove near the northern end of the ridge.

Much of the ground between these two ridges has several undulations or swales caused by natural drainage; these run north to south. The advancing Confederates had to pass over or through two fences: the first was a "crossed-post" fence with horizontal rails supported by crossed posts in an "X" configuration, while the second was a "post-and-rail" fence with vertical posts, with the ends of the horizontal rails resting in holes through the posts. The Confederates had to march across this terrain for a distance of approximately 1,290yd, or about three-quarters of a mile. As they set out, they had a front of 1½ miles, which included the gap between divisions. However, the advancing infantry became quite compressed due to oblique marching of Pickett's Division, so that the attack would actually strike a section of the Union line only 538yd in length, which was only 20 percent of the original Confederate front.

The sun was behind the Confederate lines and somewhat to the north on the day of the battle. The weather was hot, humid, and clear, although the attack produced a tremendous amount of gun-smoke.

This painting by Edwin Forbes depicts the advance of Pickett's Division on the Union center at about 15:10hrs on July 3, 1863, and illustrates the swales, or undulations, in the path of the Confederate infantry. Note the "crossed-post" fence dividing their "line of battle." (Library of Congress LC-USZC4-978)

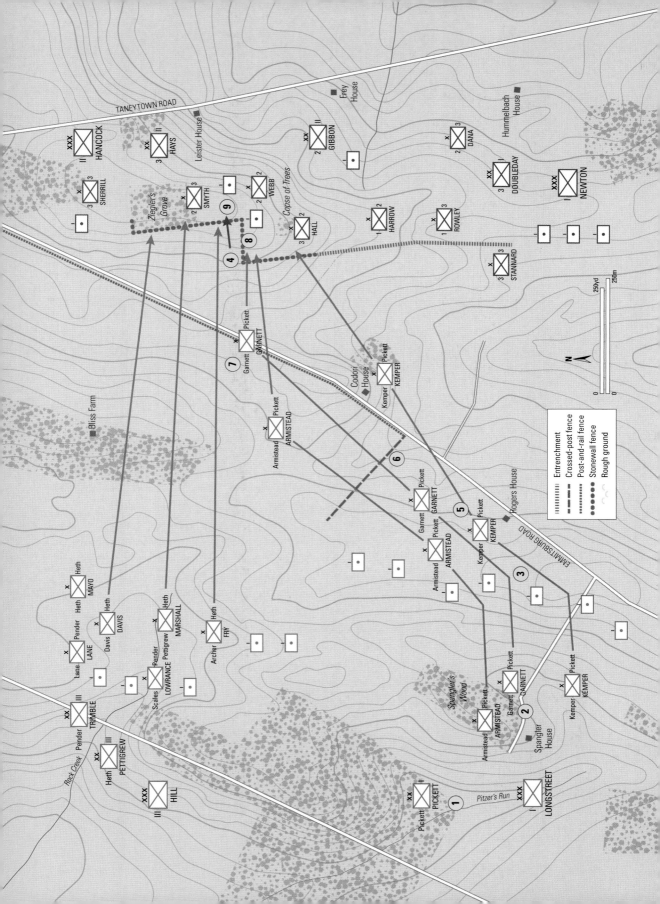

The orders to us were to advance slowly, with arms "at will," no cheering, no firing, no breaking from "common" to "quick," or "changing" step and "to dress on the center" … As we came in sight there seemed to be restlessness and excitement along the enemy's lines which encouraged some of us to hope they would not make a stubborn resistance. Their skirmishers began to run in and the artillery opened upon us all along our front. (*BEN* May 29, 1894)

The 56th Virginia had taken only a few steps beyond the Confederate artillery when Col Stuart was struck in his left side by a shell fragment. As Stuart was the only field-grade officer present with the 56th Virginia, command immediately passed to the senior captain, Capt James C. Wyant of the White Hall Guards (Co. H), although it is doubtful whether Wyant had much opportunity to exercise his new responsibility before he too was mortally wounded.

Waiting for the 56th Virginia behind a stone wall and breastworks, plus the "natural glacis" that formed that part of Cemetery Ridge, were elements of the Union II Corps, commanded by Maj Gen Winfield Scott Hancock, and part of the I Corps under Maj Gen John Newton. Although these troops amounted to only 5,750, roughly half the number of attacking Confederates, there were ample Union reserves to the right and left, and especially to the rear. Behind a minor salient in the Union center to the left of the copse of trees, which consisted of a low stone-walled fence taking an 80yd right-angle turn, and known afterward as "The Bloody Angle," was Brig Gen Alexander S. Webb's 2nd Brigade ("Philadelphia Brigade") of Brig Gen John Gibbon's Second Division, II Corps, consisting of the 69th, 71st, 72nd, and 106th Pennsylvania, totaling 940 men.

The cloudy and humid dawn found the men of the "Philadelphia Brigade" recovering from the previous day's action. Composed mainly of veterans of the Peninsula Campaign, Antietam, and Fredericksburg, many of whom were Californians, the men of the 71st Pennsylvania awoke to find they were surrounded by the wreckage of the battle. Unburied dead and mangled horses, smashed artillery equipment, and discarded muskets and accouterments littered the viciously contested acreage in front of Cemetery Ridge. With the temperature at 73 degrees Fahrenheit and rising by 07:00hrs, it was going to be another very hot day. In a letter to his parents, Sgt Albert G. Bunn of Co. B wrote, "We were awakened very early this morning, and were moved up to our present position, where we can hear the roar of the cannon" (*MDS* Aug 10, 1863: 2:5).

Commanding the 71st Pennsylvania, Col Richard Penn Smith was standing with Brig Gen Webb near the copse of trees at the extreme left wing of his regiment when the Confederates infantry marched into view to begin the attack. Webb ordered Smith to move his men up to the stone wall and to place the left of the regiment on the right wing of the 69th Pennsylvania. As the "Californians" deployed at "The Bloody Angle," Smith realized that he could not squeeze his entire command into the space on the right of the 69th:

Col Richard Penn Smith commanded the 71st Pennsylvania at Gettysburg in July of 1863. Owing to his foresight and leadership, most of the 71st Pennsylvania stood the test of fire at "The Bloody Angle." (USAMHI – RG667S-VOL.80, p. 4020, Massachusetts Commandery Military Order of the Loyal Legion)

"I could not operate at ease and satisfaction," he later explained. In consequence, he was compelled to deploy the right wing of his line in the open field just north of the east–west stone wall, which he believed was "a fearfully exposed position" (quoted in Lash 2001: 340). However, in an act of amazing foresight, he ordered detachments of his command to gather up the abandoned muskets lying close by, and had them distributed along the line and loaded. This would enable his men to fire a number of times rapidly without reloading when the enemy came within range. According to Smith, some of the men at the stone wall went into position with as many as a dozen muskets each.

Standing to the right and rear of the 71st Pennsylvania, 22-year-old Sgt Maj William S. Stockton marveled at the sight of the massed Confederate infantry heading toward the Union line. Quickly, the prone men to his front scrambled to their feet and moved down the slope toward the unoccupied segment of stone wall on the right of the 69th Pennsylvania. As this maneuver got underway, Capt William Dull, commanding Co. B, who was described in the muster roll as a "good and brave officer," was wounded in the side by a shell fragment and died shortly thereafter (quoted in Lash 2001: 340). 1/Lt John D. Rodgers, of the same company, was struck in the head and killed instantly shortly afterward. Commanding Battery A, 4th U.S. Artillery, which was posted about 26yd in the rear of the 71st Pennsylvania, 1/Lt Alonzo Cushing also requested and received permission from Brig Gen Webb to move three of his six 3in rifled guns forward to the stone wall.

In a display of what Webb later referred to as "true military intelligence on the field," and without orders, Smith next withdrew the exposed troops on the right wing of his regiment, consisting of approximately two companies of men, to the north–south-trending stone wall about 65yd to the rear, leaving Lt Col Charles Kochersperger in command of the 71st Pennsylvania's left wing at the forward stone wall (Lash 2001: 340). These troops hurried up the slope and formed behind a stretch of "dilapidated stone wall" recently abandoned by Capt William Arnold's Battery A, 1st Rhode Island Light Artillery, and on the left of the 14th Connecticut. Although the fence yielded partial protection from musketry fire, Smith believed that the neglected barrier offered little protection from Confederate artillery.

After Smith had posted his two companies in the rear, he hurried back to the main body of the 71st Pennsylvania and instructed Kochersperger to hold fire until the enemy had crossed the Emmitsburg Road, and then to "load and fire as fast as possible." He finally cautioned his lieutenant colonel to be wary of enfilading fire from the right or north of his position. Smith next ran back to his two rear companies; these men were to hold their fire until "the result with the left wing" of the regiment had been determined. If their comrades at the forward wall fell back, they were to deliver a "sure and damaging enfilading fire" into the advancing Confederates (quoted in Lash 2001: 341).

Out in the wheat fields before Cemetery Ridge, Maj Gen Pickett, with his four aides, was riding about 20yd in the rear of his division in order to observe

A pioneer of mezzotint engraving in the United States, John Sartain produced this rendition of a clash between Union and Confederate troops, possibly during Pickett's charge, at Gettysburg, Pennsylvania. (Library of Congress LC-DIG-pga-03266)

his entire command more easily. Once the Confederate lines had passed the crest of the ridge, with the clump of trees now in plain view, the Union artillery opened fire, testing the range and causing same casualties in the Confederate ranks. After a few minutes the time came to initiate the maneuver necessary in order to unite his division with that of Pettigrew. Thus, the order "left oblique!" was given, which meant that each infantryman turned 45 degrees to the left, so that the whole line sidled toward Pettigrew's without altering its general north–south alignment or faltering in its progress. Watching from Cemetery Ridge, the Union troops were deeply impressed by the parade-ground precision with which this maneuver was executed under artillery fire. Disappearing from view in the first swale, which sheltered them from most of the fire, Pickett's Division halted for several minutes to dress ranks.

As Pickett's Division recommenced its advance, the Union artillery continued its cannonade and began to cause devastation in the Confederate ranks. "This fire soon became strictly *enfilading* as we changed the point of direction from the *center* to the *left* while on the march," recalled 1/Lt Finley, "and whenever it struck our ranks was fearfully destructive." The first shell landed among the Mecklenburg Guards (Co. A), 56th Virginia, scattering them like rag dolls. 1/Lt Frank Nelson remembered, "Just before we reached the Emmitsburg Road a shell killed three and wounded three, a loss of six out of my company of only 25. Our pace was regular time" (*TD* Sep 28, 1936). A second shell landed in the Buckingham Yancey Guards (Co. D), 56th Virginia, knocking down five men, killing three and wounding two. A third shell struck the extreme right of the White Hall Guards (Co. H), numbering

37 and the largest company in the regiment; every single man was blown off his feet. While some scrambled back up, others lay still, either dead or dying. Throughout their progress toward the enemy, the whole brigade could hear Brig Gen Garnett calling as he rode at their head on his steed "Red Eye," "Steady men. Steady. Save your strength for the end." "As we neared the Emmetsburg [*sic*] road," recalled 1/Lt Finley, "the Federals behind the stone fence on the hill opened a rapid fire upon us with muskets. But as they were stooping behind that fence, I think they overshot us" (*BEN* May 29, 1894).

Behind the forward stone wall the left wing of the 71st Pennsylvania had become "hotly engaged" with the enemy on its front. "The firing had became [*sic*] general and the sharp ring of musketry and roar of cannon and thunder of bursting shells made such a deafening noise that the human voice was drowned in the din," wrote Col Smith years after the battle. The "Californians" quickly used up their ready-loaded muskets and were firing and reloading as fast as they could. Wild shouts and oaths filled the air. Even the colonel picked up a rifle and fired a few rounds. He later recalled, "I fancied that if I could at least, Chinese-like, scare [them] with noise, and I might, by accident, hit a gray-coat" (quoted in Lash 2001: 340). Even so, the Confederates continued forward.

At about this time, 1/Sgt Frederick Füger, of Cushing's battery, instructed some of the "Californians" to sight one of the guns on the road and fire just as the front-rank men of the advancing Confederate force were climbing the "post-and-rail" fence. At the appointed moment, the lanyard was pulled, sending canister on its way. "[T]he havoc caused by that overloaded gun," observed Col Smith, "scattering its deadly missiles in the enemy's ranks, was frightful, being fired at short range" (quoted in Lash 2001: 341). Commanding the 56th Virginia by this time, Capt Wyant was badly wounded in the face as a result of this blast and, following capture, died in a Union hospital on July 31, 1863.

Those Virginians that survived the blast continued to clamber over the fence and resumed their approach. Following up behind the 56th Virginia in Armistead's Brigade, 2/Lt John Lewis of Co. G, 9th Virginia, observed, "Within 800 yards of the Federal works Garnett's brigade gave their usual yell and strike the double-quick. At 100 yards they deliver their fire and dash at the works with the bayonet" (quoted in Rollins 2005: 193).

Behind the stone fence, the Union troops received a hail of musketry fire. Pvt Robert F. Wallin of Co. C, 71st Pennsylvania, suffered a mortal head wound. Pvt George W. Beidelman, of the same company, was struck by a ball that cut across both legs just above the knees. Pvt Matthew Smith of Co. G and Sgt Francis Vanderveher of Co. H both received chest wounds and were eventually carried off the field. Hit in the left leg, 27-year-old Pvt John Stockton of Co. I struggled to the rear. Just as he was aiming his musket, 19-year-old Pvt John C. Dyre of Co. E was struck by a Minié ball in the head just behind the left ear. Serving at one of the guns, Sgt Alfred Bunn of Co. B was hit in the leg and arm, but refused to leave his post, following which a third shot struck him in the head, killing him instantly.

When he was between 75yd and 100yd from the forward stone wall at "the Bloody Angle," 1/Lt Finley observed that "some of the [Union] men holding it began to break for the rear." In fact, those "Californians" on the left wing and nearest the 69th Pennsylvania did break and run. According to Finley, several of them rushed toward him, crying, "Don't shoot! We surrender! Where should we go?" (*BEN* May 29, 1894). Sgt Maj William S. Stockton, at the right of the forward line of the 71st Pennsylvania, near the apex of the outer angle, recalled seeing a few of his comrades "start for the rear" and, seemingly being unaware of Smith's order regarding falling back, "thought it rather cowardly" (quoted in Lash 2001: 343).

However, many of the men around Stockton and along the stone wall remained at their posts and offered a short but stiff hand-to-hand defense before being killed, wounded, or captured. Some of those who had helped load and fire the rifled gun used artillery tools to lunge at the first Confederates to arrive at the wall. Pvt Charles Olcott of Co. E knocked an officer down with a sponge staff. A Pennsylvania officer thrust his sword at the breast of a Tennessean captain, who just managed to parry it in time. Some "Californians," including 1/Lt Jacob S. Devine, were captured and sent across to Seminary Ridge.

By the time the remnants of the 56th Virginia reached "the Bloody Angle," every man was fighting "off his own hook." According to Union artilleryman 1/Sgt Frederick Füger, "they were not formed to a solid line, they came up in groups of fifty or a hundred … and of all those rebels that came over the stone wall not one got back" (quoted in Rollins 2005: 345). As Finley scrambled over he looked to his left, noticing for the first time "a line of troops," representing Archer's Brigade, joining the Virginians.

Meanwhile, the "Californians" still defending the wall continued to put up a stiff resistance. Pvt James Norris of Co. H, 56th Virginia, had just fired his musket when a Pennsylvanian lunged at him from behind with fixed bayonet. Whereupon, his company commander 1/Lt Henry Michie yelled a warning and the 19-year-old enlisted man whirled around and bayoneted his assailant in the stomach. Within the next few minutes Norris was a prisoner-of-war. Pvt Audubon C. Smith of Co. C, 56th Virginia, stood inside the stone wall and repeatedly loaded and fired his musket until Minié balls struck him in both shoulders, knocking him to the ground. Given water and helped off the field by a Union soldier, Smith was treated in a hospital at Chester, Pennsylvania, following which he was paroled and sent back south to Virginia. Color-bearer Pvt Alexander Williams of Co. I, 56th Virginia, also stood inside the wall waving his battle flag within 10yd of the recoiling Union lines until he was bowled over by a Minié ball in the thigh, following which a Pennsylvanian plucked the flag from his grasp and "drove him to the rear."

According to Webb, the "Californians" that did fall back were rallied by Col Smith who was assisted by Capt Frank Haskell, aide-de-camp to Brig Gen Gibbon. According to Haskell:

> I ordered these men to "halt," and "face about" and "fire," and they heard my voice and gathered my meaning, and obeyed my commands. On some unpatriotic backs of those not quick of comprehension, the flat of my sabre [sic] fell not lightly, and, at its touch their love of country returned, and, with a look at me as if I were the destroying angel … they again faced the enemy. (Haskell 2006: 61)

Although the rallied Union men formed a line on the left of the 72nd Pennsylvania, the latter regiment initially refused to advance. However, the rear wing of the 71st Pennsylvania, with their ready supply of loaded muskets, loosed an enfilade fire into the Confederates still streaming over the stone wall and up the slope. Col Smith believed that this "most galling and rapid fire" prevented the Confederates from turning Cushing's abandoned guns on the Union troops, though it is doubtful this could have happened given the shattered condition of the battery. Even so, it may have been this fire that killed Garnett outright and mortally wounded Brig Gen Armistead several yards beyond the stone wall. Certainly, the destructive crossfire delivered by Smith's right-wing companies checked the left of the Confederate penetration,

Based on a drawing by A.R. Waud, this *Harper's Weekly* engraving depicts the arrival of the troops of Pickett's Division at "The Bloody Angle" on Cemetery Ridge at Gettysburg on July 3, 1863. (Author's collection)

Photographed after capture at Gettysburg, these three Confederate infantrymen are laden with extra blanket rolls and equipage, which indicates they may have been picking up things on the battlefield to take with them as comforts in captivity. They appear to be posed in front of a Union wooden breastwork. (Library of Congress LC-DIG-cwpb-01451)

sending many if not all of the attackers reeling back. Although wounded in the leg, Webb seized the initiative and turned to the 72nd Pennsylvania, yelling, "Come up, boys, the enemy is running" (quoted in Lash 2001: 347). At the same time, reserve Union troops consisting of the 19th Massachusetts and 42nd New York, plus 20th Massachusetts, advanced through the copse of trees; this rush impelled the 72nd Pennsylvania also to move forward at last.

Somehow the Confederates managed to hold on to the stone wall at "The Bloody Angle" for a short while, hoping reinforcements would be sent to support them and waiting for the reinforced Union troops to make their final counterattack. Eventually, some realized they faced the enemy on three sides and attempted to retreat back to Seminary Ridge. Miraculously, 1/Lt Frank Nelson of Co. A, 56th Virginia, led a small group of his men back to the Confederate lines; he later recalled: "we walked away deliberately, escaping capture. They were so elated at the number of prisoners they had taken they did not bother about those on foot. It was near dark when we got back to Seminary Ridge. I brought back only five men of the 25 I had taken in, and found myself in command of the regiment" (*TD* Sep 28, 1936). Meanwhile, as the highest-ranking Confederate officer left standing at "the Bloody Angle," 1/Lt Finley of Co. K, 56th Virginia, at last gave the order to surrender. "Seeing that it was a useless waste of life to struggle longer I ordered the few men around me to 'cease firing' and surrendered. Others to the right and left did the same, and soon the sharp quick huzza! of the Federals told of our defeat and their triumph" (*BEN* May 29, 1894).

Chaffin's Farm/ New Market Heights

September 29, 1864

BACKGROUND TO BATTLE

Lee retreated back into Virginia after his defeat at Gettysburg, and offered his resignation to Jefferson Davis, which was refused. The rest of 1863 passed without a major battle between the two armies in Virginia. Late in 1863 a cavalry expedition under Brig Gen Judson Kilpatrick attempted to capture Richmond, but this failed and no further significant fighting took place until the spring of 1864.

Following great success in the Western Theater of the war, Ulysses S. Grant had been made lieutenant general and commander of all of the Union Armies on March 9, 1864. Heading east, he turned his attention to operations south of the James River in mid-June, having been repeatedly blocked with heavy losses by Lee during various efforts to capture Richmond during his overland campaign in Virginia, which involved battles at the Wilderness, Spotsylvania Court House, North Anna, and Cold Harbor. His main objective south of the James was Petersburg, which served as a major supply artery, inland port, and railroad hub for the Confederacy. Following failure to capture Petersburg during his assault of June 15–18, Grant began a prolonged siege of Petersburg, which would last until finally broken on April 2, 1865 following the Union victory at Five Forks.

On several occasions Grant attempted to divert Confederate attention away from the Petersburg defenses by attacking the lines protecting Richmond. If successful, these actions may even have captured the Confederate capital. The third of these operations occurred on September 29, 1864. The strike force for this attack was Maj Gen Benjamin Butler's Army of the James. During the night of September 28/29, 1864, Butler's troops crossed the James, and conducted

Photographed at Fortress Monroe, Virginia, in October of 1863, Maj Augustus S. Boernstein was the only field-grade officer of the 4th USCT present during the assault on Chaffin's Farm/ New Market Heights on September 29, 1864. (Christian A. Fleetwood Papers, Manuscript Division, Library of Congress)

a two-pronged dawn attack on the Confederate right and center. The XVIII Corps under Maj Gen Edward O.C. Ord crossed the James to Aiken's Landing by a newly constructed pontoon bridge. The X Corps under Maj Gen David B. Birney, followed by the Cavalry Division under Brig Gen August V. Kautz, went over via the Deep Bottom pontoon bridge.

Forming the right wing of the assault, Birney's corps, augmented by a USCT division under the inexperienced Brig Gen Charles J. Paine from the XVIII Corps, would advance in a northwesterly direction to assault the Confederate line running along the south side of the New Market Road near Chaffin's Farm. If successful they would drive on to capture the artillery positions behind it on New Market Heights. This action would protect the left wing of the Union attack, which would attempt to capture Fort Harrison, a strong point on that part of the Confederate line. If this operation succeeded and New Market Heights were seized, Kautz's cavalry could push on and attack Fort Gilmer, about 1½ miles beyond on the inner line of defenses, and possibly capture Richmond. Beginning just before dawn, the Union attack was to be spearheaded by the African American troops of Col Samuel A. Duncan's 3rd Brigade, consisting of only about 750 men of the 4th and 6th USCT, which was significantly less than the strength of a single early-war regiment. The inexperienced third regiment of this brigade, the 10th USCT, had been left behind at City Point, Virginia.

The Confederate line in front of New Market Heights was held by about 2,000 veteran troops thinly spread along the trenches under the overall command of Brig Gen John Gregg, of Alabama. Lt Col Frederick Bass's under-strength Texas Brigade consisted of the 1st, 4th, and 5th Texas, plus the 3rd Arkansas. Becoming known as Lee's "Grenadier Guard," it served throughout the war within Longstreet's First Corps and participated in at least 24 battles in 1862, including Eltham's Landing, Gaines' Mill, Second Bull Run/Manassas, and Sharpsburg. In 1863 it saw further action at Gettysburg, Chickamauga, and the siege of Chattanooga. Much reduced in numbers by September of 1864, this brigade was stretched so thinly along the trench line at Chaffin's Farm that gaps existed in many places.

To the Texas Brigade's right was the dismounted cavalry brigade commanded by Brig Gen Martin Gary, composed of the 24th Virginia Cavalry, 7th South Carolina Cavalry, and the Hampton Legion. Artillery support was provided by the five guns of Capt Archibald Graham's 1st Rockbridge Artillery on New Market Heights and 1/Lt Henry C. Carter's two 3in Rifles of the 3rd Richmond Howitzers, posted left of the Texas Brigade.

INTO COMBAT

Just before the cold light of dawn revealed the ground fog in front of the Confederate trenches at Chaffin's Farm/New Market Heights on September 29, 1864, orders arrived via a courier from Brig Gen Paine to

Col Duncan, and the 3rd Brigade was sent forward. The USCT troops were to fight in light marching order and, besides their normal equipment, had only a single blanket rolled and carried over the shoulder. According to Sgt Maj Christian A. Fleetwood, 4th USCT, "Our regiment lined up for the charge with eleven officers and 350 enlisted men. There was but one field officer with us, Major Augustus S. Boernstein who was in command [as their regimental commander led the brigade]. Our adjutant, First Lieutenant George Allen, supervised the right, and I, as sergeant-major, the left" (quoted in Beyer 1905: 434).

At about 05:20hrs, Maj Gen Butler rode up to the troops to exhort them. He later recalled that he found the USCT troops "with guns at 'right shoulder shift,'" which indicated that they were ready to step off. Unusually, and fatally, there was to be no artillery support as the Confederate line was to be taken to some extent by the element of surprise. Pointing at the New Market Line, Butler shouted, "That work must be taken by the weight of your column; no shot must be fired" (quoted in Williams 1888: 254). To ensure that this command was obeyed, he ordered the officers to ensure that their men removed the percussion caps from their muskets. Thus, they would have to rush across the open ground and capture the Confederate works at the point of the bayonet, after which they would be permitted to cap their muskets and open fire. Ironically, they were each issued an extra 20 rounds of ammunition, which they probably carried in their haversacks. To make matters worse, only a few men detailed as pioneers were equipped with axes and hatchets with which to hew out an opening in the wooden barriers protecting the approaches to the trench line.

Butler then sought to lift the spirits of his troops by reminding those nearby who could hear him that it was their duty to avenge the recent massacre of African American infantrymen in Tennessee earlier that year: "Your cry, when you charge, will be, 'Remember Fort Pillow!'" (quoted in Williams 1888: 254). The massacre of the African American garrison of Fort Pillow, a Union bastion on the Mississippi River on April 12, 1864, provided Duncan's brigade with much reason for revenge.

Finally, at about 05:30hrs, Duncan bellowed "Forward!" and according to Capt John McMurray of Co. D, 6th USCT, "as one man we plunged into the slashing." As they set off, Duncan described his men disappearing "as they entered the fog that enwrapped them like the mantle of death." Formed in "open column of companies," the 4th USCT led the way, preceded by a line of skirmishers, with Maj Boernstein following on horseback about 35 paces (22yd) behind the file closers of the rear company. The 6th USCT followed in echelon toward the left rear, with its commander, Col Ames, and Duncan following behind. Shortly after the action, Boernstein wrote, "We did not dismount during the whole fight until our horses were shot" (quoted in Price 2011: 59).

As Duncan's brigade advanced, Paine made a blunder that would cause his African American troops to sustain very high casualties. Instead of

1 05:20hrs (approx.): Col Samuel A. Duncan's 3rd Brigade, Third Division, XVIII Corps, Army of the James, consisting of the 4th and 6th USCT, is assembled northwest of Deep Bottom for the attack on the Confederate line at Chaffin's Farm/ New Market Heights.

2 05:30hrs (approx.): The African American troops are ordered forward in "open column of companies," with the 4th USCT leading the way and the 6th USCT following in left echelon, or slightly behind and to the left.

3 05:35hrs (approx.): As they reach the Kingsland Road, both USCT regiments recall skirmishers and deploy into "line of battle."

4 05:40hrs (approx.): The Confederate pickets of the Texas Brigade see the Union troops looming out of the fog, warn of the approaching attack, and withdraw to the main defenses.

5 05:40hrs (approx.): With the aid of observers in the signal tower behind their lines, who probably relayed news of the approaching attack via telegraph, Confederate infantry is massed in the trenches at the point approached by the Union troops. Confederate artillery on Cobb's Hill opens fire at close range in hopes of hitting the fog-enshrouded enemy.

6 05:40hrs (approx.): The order to "charge bayonets" is given by brigade commander Col Samuel A. Duncan, and passed down via regimental, battalion and company commanders, and the African American troops dash toward the Confederate line.

7 05:42hrs (approx.): As they tumble across Four Mile Creek, the Union troops receive a hail of Confederate musketry fire. The flags of both USCT regiments are saved and continue to wave.

8 05:45hrs (approx.): A few white officers and African American troops of the USCT fight through the abatis and *fraise* and reach the Confederate trench line. Many are shot down or bayoneted.

9 05:50hrs (approx.): Realizing the futility of their situation, the surviving Union infantrymen scramble back over the stream and fall back toward Deep Bottom, leaving 280 dead and wounded on the battlefield.

Battlefield environment

By 1864 the nature of warfare had changed significantly and infantry attempting to advance on the enemy faced a host of field fortifications manned by troops largely armed with rifle-muskets, offering a deadly accurate fire that made frontal assault a highly risky strategy. In order to approach the Chaffin's Farm/New Market Heights line, the African American volunteers of Butler's Army of the James had to cross a rising plain extending about 500yd toward a swampy branch of Four Mile Creek. Beyond this lay a deep, heavily wooded ravine that ran parallel to the New Market Road, the other side of which was another plain of about 300yd rising northward toward that road. The latter area was covered with field fortifications consisting of a double line of abatis, also known as "slashings," composed of felled trees with tangled branches pointing toward the enemy. Beyond this was a line of outward projecting palisade called *fraise*, and 16yd farther on was the earthworks consisting of a breastwork about 5ft high with a 10ft-deep ditch in front. However, dense fog would hide the attacking Union force until it was about 33yd from the Confederate line.

This *Harper's Weekly* engraving shows Union troops of Ord's XVIII Corps capturing Fort Harrison, to the west of Chaffin's Farm. The attack of the 4th and 6th USCT would serve as a diversion for this action. (Author's collection)

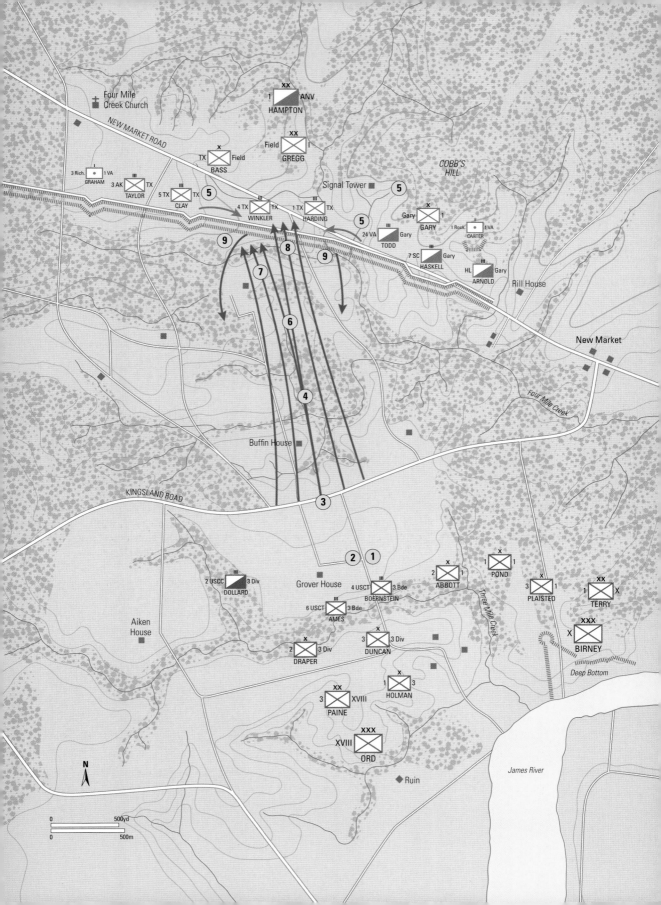

Four Mile Creek Church

NEW MARKET ROAD

xx
1 ANV
HAMPTON

xx
Field I
GREGG

x
TX Field
BASS

COBB'S HILL

3 Rich. 1 VA
GRAHAM

III
3 AK TX
TAYLOR

III
5 TX TX
CLAY

⑤

Signal Tower

⑤

III
4 TX TX
WINKLER

III
1 TX TX
HARDING

⑤

x
Gary 1
GARY

1 Rock. 1 VA
CARTER

24 VA Gary
III
TODD

⑨

⑧

⑦

⑨

7 SC Gary
III
HASKELL

HL Gary
III
ARNOLD

Rill House

New Market

⑥

Four Mile Creek

④

Buffin House

③

KINGSLAND ROAD

②①

Grover House

III
2 USCC 3 Div
DOLLARD

III
4 USCT 3 Bde
BOERNSTEIN

x
2 1
ABBOTT

x
1
POND

x
1
PLAISTED

xx
1 X
TERRY

Aiken House

III
6 USCT 3 Bde
AMES

x
3 3 Div
DUNCAN

Three Mile Creek

xxx
X
BIRNEY

x
2 3 Div
DRAPER

Deep Bottom

x
1 3
HOLMAN

xx
3 XVIII
PAINE

xxx
XVIII
ORD

James River

Ruin

N

0   500yd
0   500m

Photographed at Fort Lincoln in Washington, D.C., on November 17, 1865, standing at "Parade – Rest" as per Casey's *Infantry Tactics*, many of these enlisted men of Co. E, 4th USCT, had seen hard fighting at Chaffin's Farm/New Market Heights during the previous year. Typical of African American troops, they are well uniformed and wear full-dress brass shoulder scales on their frock coats. The two non-commissioned officers at left wear either cavalry- or light-artillery-pattern jackets which appear to be devoid of branch service trim of yellow or scarlet respectively on collar and cuffs. (Library of Congress LC-B817- 7890)

ensuring that they continued to push northwest once they had crossed the Kingsland Road, where they would have encountered fewer obstacles and could have isolated the Confederates manning the New Market Line east of Four Mile Creek, he ordered them north. This ensured that they had to cross the boggy creek only a few hundred yards from the Confederate line before they reached the extensive field fortifications. At the same time, the other two brigades under Paine's command remained inactive: Draper received no further orders to advance his 2nd Brigade in support, and he had his men lie down near the Buffin House, while Holman's 1st Brigade remained static well behind Duncan. In fact the only support eventually received came from a detachment of the 2nd U.S. Colored Cavalry, which had been detailed as sharpshooters of the Third Division, XVIII Corps, and were deployed on Duncan's left.

Meanwhile, when the 4th USCT reached the Kingsland Road, about halfway toward the Confederate lines, the skirmishers of the two flank companies were recalled and the regiment was deployed in "line of battle." Although about 400yd away from the Confederate trenches and so not

within musket range of the main body of enemy infantry, the regiment began to receive fire from the Confederate pickets. Furthermore, shells from the Confederate artillery to their right and left began to scream overhead to burst in their rear as the gunners tested their range. As the sun slowly burned through the dense ground fog, the long blue lines of the 4th and 6th USCT began to emerge from the mists. Withdrawing back into their main line, the Confederate pickets warned their compatriots of the approaching enemy.

Commanding the 4th Texas, Lt Col Clinton M. Winkler had been enjoying a brief respite with his wife at the nearby Phillips House when firing on the picket line was heard. Angelina Winkler recalled her husband "hastily bidding me good-bye [with] sharpshooting beginning to be heard" (Winkler 1894: 192). In the trenches, the Confederate defenders put down their coffee, picked up their muskets and, peering into the gray half-light of dawn, searched for their targets. Using the signal tower to their rear, the regimental officers were able to concentrate the thinly stretched troops at the point in the trench line most vulnerable to the approaching assault.

Christian Fleetwood, 4th USCT

The highest enlisted rank in either a Union or Confederate infantry regiment was that of sergeant major. Selected by the regimental commander, one of the sergeant major's many tasks involved assisting the regimental adjutant in the performance of his duties in camp. Considered to be a model soldier for the rest of the regiment in his dress and military deportment, the example he set influenced proper discipline in the unit.

Like most of the soldiers of the 4th USCT, Sgt Maj Christian A. Fleetwood was recruited in Maryland. Born in Baltimore on July 21, 1840, he was the son of Charles and Anna Maria Fleetwood, both free persons of color. During August of 1863, Fleetwood enlisted for three years in Co. G, 4th USCT, and as an educated man was soon promoted to sergeant major. Assigned to the Third Division, Fleetwood's regiment saw service with the X, XVIII, and XXV Corps in campaigns in North Carolina and Virginia.

In preparation for the assault on Chaffin's Farm/ New Market Heights on September 29, 1864, it was his duty as sergeant major to post the left guide, or marker, and after all the companies had been formed in "line of battle," he was to place himself two paces on the extreme left of the regiment. Serving as an example to the rest of the regiment, he then urged it forward during the attack, and ensured that the regiment's National flag continued to wave. Having served with distinction at Chaffin's Farm/New Market Heights, Fleetwood would be one of 17 officers and men who took part in that action to be awarded for their bravery with the Congressional Medal of Honor.

LEFT Christian A. Fleetwood wears civilian clothes in the *carte de visite* taken in Baltimore, Maryland, before he enlisted. (Christian A. Fleetwood Papers, Manuscript Division, Library of Congress)

RIGHT Photographed at Fort Slocum, Washington, D.C., in October of 1865, Sgt Maj Christian Fleetwood wears his Medal of Honor (left) and the Medal for Colored Troops issued for valor displayed at Chaffin's Farm/New Market Heights by Maj Gen Benjamin Butler (right). The latter was cast by Tiffany & Company and modelled after medallions issued by Queen Victoria during the Crimean War. His rank of sergeant major is indicated by three chevrons and an arc on the sleeves of his coat. It is not known who the young boy was. (Library of Congress LC-USZ62-107713 detail)

Writing several days after the action, Brig Gen Paine marveled in a letter home that "there were not many men in the Reb line … but where I assaulted there were as many as the works w[oul]d hold. They had a signal tower which overlooked everything and [which] enabled them to concentrate to meet me" (quoted in Price 2011: 60).

Of the approaching attack, 18-year-old Pvt Orlando T. Hanks of the Texas Invincibles (Co. K), 1st Texas, remembered:

One beautiful still morning about sunrise we heard cheering in the distance on the James [River]. It was so faint it sounded like little school boys at play. We were preparing our breakfast and did not pay much attention to it. I was boiling for myself and mess, a pot of sweet potatoes. Just then the hieing was nearer. Some of the boys remarked that those wretches were coming one and all on us. Twas but a little while our pickets began to pup away and gave them a pretty stiff fight. But it was of no use. They were being driven by a strong line of battle of the enemy. By this time our officers began to give orders to fall in line and get

Clinton M. Winkler, 4th Texas

Like so many Southerners who served as officers in the Confederate Army, Clinton Winkler was by profession an "attorney-at-law" when he was elected captain commanding the Navarro Rifles (Co. I), 4th Texas Volunteer Infantry, Hood's Brigade, in 1861. Born in Burke County, North Carolina, on October 19, 1821, Winkler migrated with his parents to Indiana in 1835. Aged 18 he determined to move to Texas, where he settled in Franklin, Robertson County, in July of 1840. He took an active part in frontier life and joined numerous expeditions to track down marauding Native Americans, which provided him with valuable pre-war military experience.

A competent junior officer, Winkler led his company through Civil War battles at Eltham's Landing, Gaines Mill, Second Bull Run/Manassas, and South Mountain in 1862, and was severely wounded at Gettysburg on July 2 during the Confederate attack on Little Round Top. As with many other junior officers in the Confederate Army, he rapidly rose through the ranks as others were killed or mortally wounded. While recovering from his Gettysburg wound, he was promoted to major on July 21, 1863, and on August 10, 1864, received the rank of lieutenant colonel, commanding the 4th Texas at New Market Heights/Chaffin's Farm on September 29 of the same year.

In battle the regimental commander would normally have been mounted and riding at a short distance behind his troops. With his command entrenched at Chaffin's Farm/New Market Heights, Lt Col Winkler was probably posted at the center of his regiment with aides and couriers or runners close-by poised to relay commands.

Winkler temporarily commanded the brigade after Brig Gen John Gregg was killed in the Richmond defenses on October 9, 1864, and surrendered in command of the remains of the 4th Texas at Appomattox on April 4, 1865.

In 1861 Clinton M. Winkler recruited and led the Navarro Rifles (Co. I), 4th Texas Infantry, and rose through the ranks to command the regiment by 1864. The two stars on his collar indicate the rank of lieutenant colonel. (Texas Heritage Museum, Hill College, Texas)

into the breastworks. Into them we went. I carried my pot of potatoes. I had not time to eat them and less appetite. Likewise I left them sitting there and they are there now as far as I know. (Quoted in Price 2011: 59–60)

Sgt Edward R. Crockett of Co. F, 4th Texas, commented more simply in his diary, "The 29th, Thursday, all up and under arms at 4 o'clock, at early dawn. The rifles began to crack on the picket line … All is excitement now" (quoted in Price 2011: 54).

At about 05:40hrs Duncan ordered his brigade to charge. With a shout that rippled along its entire length, the Union battle line surged forward at "Charge – Bayonets," with each man trying to keep abreast of the color guard. The Confederates mostly held their fire as the African American troops crossed the open field toward the wooded ravine concealing the creek. Some jumped, others tumbled, into the ravine they had not detected on their approach. Most scrambled up through the trees on the opposite bank, while the less fortunate, such as brothers Joseph H. Bantum (Co. G) and Robert Bantum (Co. H), tumbled back into the muddy water, cut down by the hail of Minié balls and shells that now greeted them. Rallying and regaining a foothold on level ground, those Union soldiers that remained raced up toward the double line of abatis.

Forming in the trenches and rifle pits, the Texans and Arkansans awaited the as yet unseen enemy. They could distinctly hear the Union officers, as in loud tones they gave such commands as were needed to keep their men moving, but until the African American troops approached within 30yd, could see nothing except a wavering dark line. As the Union troops became more visible, the Confederates sprang to the top of the low breastworks, and commenced firing, "shooting at shadows," as one of them recalled.

Fleetwood was still leading the remains of the left wing of the 4th USCT. He later recalled:

> When the charge was started our color-guard was complete. Only one of the twelve came off that field on his own feet. Most of the others are there still. Early in the rush one of the sergeants went down, a bullet cutting his flag-staff in two and passing through his body. The other sergeant, Alfred B. Hilton, of Company H, a magnificent specimen of manhood, over six feet tall and splendidly proportioned, caught up the other flag and pressed forward with them both. (Quoted in Beyer 1905: 434)

By this time, the Union line of battle had disintegrated and communication between officers and men had completely broken down. "It was a deadly hailstorm of bullets, sweeping men down as hailstones sweep the leaves from the trees," remembered Fleetwood. It was not long before Sgt Hilton also went down, shot through the right leg. As he fell he held up the flags and shouted, "Boys, save the colors!" (quoted in Beyer 1905: 434). Before they could touch the ground, Cpl Charles Veal of Co. D had seized the regimental flag, and Fleetwood grabbed the National flag.

As the 6th USCT made its final approach to the Confederate line, the regimental adjutant, 1/Lt Nathan Edgerton, found great difficulty maneuvering through the swampy terrain on horseback. Of his approach to the streambed, he recalled, "I jumped from my horse and threw the reins to the orderly, for I was sure the horse would be unable to get across owing to the marshy nature of the ground. The reins had hardly left my hand when the horse went down, shot dead from the opposite bank." Struggling across on foot, he found "a level space of ground thickly covered with … dead and wounded" (quoted in Price 2011: 61). Among the carnage, he discovered the body of 2/Lt Frederick Meyers (Co. B) with the regimental flag still gripped in his lifeless fingers. Of further efforts to rally his men, Edgerton recollected:

> All at once I went down, but jumped up immediately and tried to raise the flag, for I thought I had fallen over the dewberry vines which grew thickly there, but

… found my hand was covered in blood, and perfectly powerless, and the flag staff lying in two pieces. I sheathed my sword, took the flag with its broken staff and reached the abatis. (The Sable Arm website)

Nearby, 1/Sgt Alexander Kelly of Co. F, 6th USCT, also saved his regiment's National flag after the color-bearer and most of Kelly's company had been either killed or wounded. For their bravery that day, Sgt Maj Fleetwood, Sgt Hilton, and 1/Sgt Kelly, plus Cpl Veal and 1/Lt Edgerton, would all receive the Medal of Honor.

Reaching the first line of abatis, those men of the 4th USCT armed with axes and hatchets hacked away at the tangled barrier while others tore at it with their bare hands while Minié balls zipped around them. Officers and men slipped through whatever gaps were made and rushed toward the second line, which a small number also managed to penetrate. Despite the order to charge, the few dozen men who got through the abatis unwounded dropped to the ground in an effort to avoid the intense Confederate fire. Noting the halt, men farther to the rear also stopped, and some ran back to the near side of the outer abatis where they crouched, attempting to take stock of the situation. At this point the surviving officers, including 2/Lt William Appleton of Co. H, urged the men back on their feet in order to regain the momentum of the attack. Most of them responded, although some held back oblivious to the shouts and gestures. Included in the latter was 1/Sgt Thomas S. Kelly of Co. C, who was subsequently reduced to the ranks.

Incredibly, a small number of USCT men managed to reach the trenches, but most were shot down at point-blank range or bayoneted to death. Several African Americans attempted to surrender but these were also killed. Indeed, Confederate accounts admit the latter. In the trenches with the Three Creek Rifles (Co. G), 3rd Arkansas, Capt Alexander C. Jones recollected:

Photographed earlier in 1864 at the Washington, D.C. studio of Alex Gardener, all three of these officers of the 4th USCT were either killed or wounded. At left, Capt Samuel W. Vannings (Co. E) was killed during the attack at Chaffin's Farm/ New Market Heights. At center, 1/Lt Thomas H. Price (Co. E) was wounded in the left hand during the same attack, which put him out of action for about seven weeks, after which he returned to duty. At right, Capt Albert G. Crawford (Co. H) was wounded in the left thigh near Petersburg on July 10, 1864. (Christian A. Fleetwood Papers, Manuscript Division, Library of Congress)

> … we had scarcely time to seize our arms and take position in the trenches when we were suddenly charged by a large body of negro troops led by white officers. These fellows seemed to follow their leaders blindly and rushed up to the very muzzles of our guns … The struggle … lasted only a few minutes, when, being apparently seized with a sudden panic, the negroes broke and scattered to the winds, leaving in our hands a few prisoners and a large number of dead and wounded on the ground, while we [3rd Arkansas] had not lost a man. (*CV* 25.1: 24–25)

During these desperate moments the black troops showed impressive discipline but understandably broke and ran, which was mistaken by the Confederates as blind obedience and then panic. Maj Boernstein, 4th USCT, recalled, "If we had succeeded in taking the Rebel line we would

"Remember Fort Pillow!"

Union view: The black infantry of the 4th USCT crash through abatis, or outer field fortifications composed of felled trees, in the last stage of their attack on the Confederate line at Chaffin's Farm/New Market Heights during the early hours of September 29, 1864. In light marching order including blanket rolls, canteens and haversacks, they were ordered by Maj Gen Butler not to cap their Model 1863 Springfield rifle-muskets, but to complete the charge with fixed bayonets only. To avenge the massacre of African American troops at Fort Pillow, a Union fort on the Mississippi River earlier that year, they were also encouraged to use the battle cry "Remember Fort Pillow!" Ahead can be seen a line of *fraise*, or outward-pointing stakes, which formed a further barrier in front of the Confederate trenches. Only a handful of the 350 African American infantrymen, and 11 white officers, of the 4th USCT reached part of the Confederate line, which they held for a few desperate minutes before being ordered to fall back. By the end of this action, nearly half the regiment had been killed, wounded, or reported missing and presumed captured.

Confederate view: Waiting in the Confederate trench line, the infantrymen of Hood's "Old Texas Brigade" armed with a mixture of Springfield and Enfield rifle-muskets open fire on the African American troops as they loom out of the early morning mist. Their trench is protected by an earthen parapet topped with pinned head-logs forming firing slits. Wooden supports called skids span the width of the trench to catch the head-log if it happened to be struck by artillery fire, sending it rolling over the heads of the defenders manning the firing step. Although the trenches at Chaffin's Farm/New Market Heights were normally thinly defended due to dwindling Confederate forces, observers in the signal tower on Cobb's Hill warned of the oncoming attack via telegraph and enabled Lt Col Frederick Bass to concentrate his troops where they were most needed. Regarding the action as a "turkey shoot," several defenders stand above the parapet to take better aim. Having been driven in from the picket line, several men are shown scrambling back into the trench. The 2,000-strong Texas Brigade sustained only one man killed and two wounded during this action.

have been captured, every one of us" (quoted in Price 2011: 59). Fleetwood later wrote:

> It was very evident that there was too much work cut out for our regiments. Strong earthworks, protected in front by two lines of abatis and one line of palisades, and in the rear by a lot of men who proved that they knew how to shoot and largely outnumbered us. We struggled through the two lines of abatis, a few getting through the palisades, but it was sheer madness, and those of us who were able I had to get out as best we could. (Quoted in Beyer 1905: 434–35)

Similar events occurred when the 6th USCT reached the abatis. Rallying those few men who appeared out of the fog and powder smoke, Col Ames yelled to those who could hear him, "We must have more help, boys, before we try that. Fall back" (quoted in Price 2011: 64). As they scrambled back over the stream and out of the pall of powder smoke, the African American troops could see how badly their under-strength brigade had been cut to pieces. The 4th USCT sustained 27 killed, 137 wounded, and 14 missing and presumed captured. The 6th USCT lost 41 killed, 160 wounded, and eight captured or missing.

The following day, Lt Col Winkler wrote his wife, who narrowly managed to escape capture during the battle, "We had a nice fight yesterday, and whipped our part of it handsomely … The enemy suffered severely; our losses trifling. The sight I witnessed of dead negroes and white Federal officers was sickening in the extreme" (Winkler 1894: 194). In fact, the Confederates sustained one man killed and two wounded. Pvt Joseph Alsbrook of the Lone Star Rifles (Co. L), 1st Texas, was bayoneted to death when the USCT troops reached the breastwork, while Pvt William T. Blackburn and Pvt Drew F. Morgan, both of the Texas Aides (Co. I), 5th Texas, were wounded – the former being captured and the latter subsequently dying of several days later.

Despite their severe losses, the 4th and 6th USCT had spearheaded an attack on the New Market Line which was followed up about two hours later by a more successful, if equally bloody, attack by the African American troops of Col Alonzo Draper's 2nd Brigade, and Col John H. Holman's 1st Brigade, Third Division, XVIII Corps. These two assaults initially drew battle-hardened Confederate infantry away from Fort Harrison, a strongpoint near Chaffin's Bluff, on the James River, and eventually forced them to abandon their trenches and withdraw to the Intermediate Line of defenses protecting the Confederate capital. Defended by inexperienced Local Defense Troops, Fort Harrison was captured later that day by the white troops of the First and Second divisions, X Corps, commanded by Brig Gen Alfred Terry and Robert Foster. Although the Union advance was stopped by the forts on the intermediate defenses, this success forced Lee to launch a series of Confederate counterattacks the next day, all of which failed to re-capture the fort.

Analysis & Conclusion

FIRST BULL RUN/MANASSAS

An examination of three examples of infantry action indicates that the role of the infantryman, and the capability of his commander, changed considerably during the course of the Civil War. At First Bull Run/Manassas in 1861, Brig Gen McDowell and most divisional officers had little idea how to handle large numbers of troops. Although the flanking attack Mc Dowell devised on July 21, 1861, may have had more chance of success if conducted by an experienced army, once the Union column finally crossed Sudely Ford and arrived on the left flank of Beauregard's line behind Bull Run, it was thrown into the fray virtually a regiment at a time rather than utilizing the brigade structure in which it was organized. The advance of the 11th New York is just one example in a series of single-regiment infantry attacks that failed to penetrate the hastily re-deployed combined forces of Beauregard and Johnston. Certainly, the drill book did not desert some of the Fire Zouave officers, who ordered "Firing by rank" to repel a cavalry charge on Henry House Hill, but much of the remainder of their performance lacked discipline if it was not short on bravery.

On the other hand, the Confederate high command, consisting of Beauregard and Johnston, marshaled and moved their troops more efficiently, with those under the latter general swiftly negotiating a distance of about 60 miles in 36 hours moving from the Shenandoah Valley to Manassas Junction via foot and railroad. At brigade level, Confederate commanders such as Thomas J. Jackson showed considerable skill in conducting their infantry, and the crucial counterattack of his brigade on Henry House Hill turned the tide of the battle. However, at regimental level matters were not so straightforward as Col A.C. Cummings, commanding the 33rd Virginia, incurred the initial wrath of his brigade commander due to his premature, if decisive, attack on the 11th New York. Clearly, brigade commanders did not expect their regimental commanders to show initiative in the early part of the Civil War.

In both armies, the raw militiamen and volunteers with only a few weeks of drill and training, and under fire for the first time, behaved as one might expect. Those handled well by their officers showed great courage but, when confronted by large numbers of enemy, were inclined to run or disobey orders. As a result of their circuitous flanking march, the Union infantry were badly dehydrated and exhausted and particularly prone to panic and retreat by the time they went into battle. The Confederate infantrymen, and particularly those who had arrived from the Shenandoah Valley the day before the battle, were equally unable to consolidate their victory by pursuing the retreating Union Army later in the day.

"THE BLOODY ANGLE," GETTYSBURG

Although there was limited use of field fortification and entrenchment on July 21, 1861, particularly by the Confederate forces dug in behind Bull Run, this aspect of warfare had developed extensively by 1863 and played its part in the infantry action at Gettysburg. Felling trees and building them into a log fence, which was battened with cord wood from piles nearby, the Union troops surmounted them with "head-logs" that later proved of inestimable value in the close-quarter infantry combat that was to follow. The Pennsylvanians at "The Bloody Angle" were for the most part defending a combination of stone-wall and wooden fence which, in their raised position, gave them a major advantage during the events of July 3. However, placing infantry behind such fortifications does not guarantee an entirely effective performance. The fact that many Union infantrymen aimed too high during Pickett's Charge, as observed by 1/Lt George Finley, 56th Virginia, indicates they feared exposing their heads above the breastworks. This is corroborated by 1/Lt Frank Nelson of the same regiment, who stated:

> If the [Union] infantry behind the stone wall had fired properly not a single Confederate would have reached it. To take aim a man had to lift his head above that structure which meant almost sure death. That the firing was bad was proved by the fact that General Garnett, a very tall man, mounted on a horse 16 hands [5ft 4in] was shot in the forehead. (*TD* Sep 28, 1936)

From the Confederate perspective, no matter how outdated and flawed Lee's grand frontal assault may have seemed, the officers involved made spectacular use of the drill book in order to marshal their troops. The parade-ground precision of the "left oblique" maneuver conducted by

The flags carried by infantry regiments in both Union and Confederate armies served as rallying points for men in battle. Only remnants of the silk National flag presented to the 4th USCT by the African American ladies of Baltimore, Maryland, survive today. Saved by Sgt Maj Christian Fleetwood during the Union attack on Chaffin's Farm/ New Market Heights on September 29, 1864, it was holed by more than 22 musket balls and its staff was cut in half. (Maryland Historical Society 2004.22)

This group of mainly USCT was photographed recuperating at Aiken's Landing, on the north side of the James River, in November of 1864 following action at Chaffin's Farm/New Market Heights. Typical of African American troops, many of them are well equipped with overcoats and knapsacks. (Library of Congress LC-DIG-cwpb-02032)

Pickett's division in the face of devastating cannon fire as they began their advance from Seminary Ridge was straight out of Hardee's manual and indicated how well drilled and disciplined his infantry was on July 3, 1863. Although the movement of infantry to both the right and left oblique must have seen considerable usage throughout the Civil War, it was reported in the *Official Records* on only a few other occasions.

The infantryman in both armies had learned to become more versatile under fire during the course of the war. Compare the lack of ability of the raw volunteers of the 11th New York at First Bull Run/Manassas with how the Pennsylvanians behaved on Cemetery Ridge. Having helped re-take the guns of Rickett's battery on Henry House Hill, the Fire Zouaves lacked the ability to use them in order to hold back the fateful advance of "Stonewall" Jackson's brigade. Albeit aided by an artillerist, the men of the 71st Pennsylvania at "The Bloody Angle" were able to man and fire one of the remaining 3in rifled guns with devastating effect. Infantrymen also became more adept at engineering tasks and constructing field fortifications such as breastworks, trenches, and rifle pits.

Much has been written about Lee's decision-making on the third day at Gettysburg and due attention has been paid to the fact that he was still recovering from the heart attack he experienced during March of 1863, which may have affected his judgement and performance later that July. However, Longstreet was not the only officer under his command to see the futility of the frontal assault Lee ordered on the Union center on the third day of battle. Surviving that action, 1/Lt Nelson, 56th Virginia, wrote, "Had we taken Cemetery Hill (the object of the attack), we could never have held it. Those who reached the stone wall saw the Federal reserves in countless thousands in the rear of the defending line. Our failure to a great extent can be laid to General Lee's one fault – he left too much to his subordinate officers" (*TD* Sep 28, 1936).

CHAFFIN'S FARM/NEW MARKET HEIGHTS

The Union attack on the Confederate lines at Chaffin's Farm/New Market Heights by the 4th and 6th USCT was a late-war example of the use of swift light-infantry tactics set forth in Hardee's manual. This particular attack failed due to the ineptitude of the divisional commander Brig Gen Charles Paine, who failed to send in support troops. The order not to cap muskets also contributed to its failure and indicates that Maj Gen Butler did not trust his African American troops to hold their fire long enough for the element of surprise to succeed. As at First Bull Run/Manassas in 1861, the Confederate commanders at Chaffin's Farm/New Market Heights made very effective use of their signalling system in order to track the movement of Union forces. Sharp-eyed lookouts in the signal tower on Cob's Hill enabled officers to gather and direct their thinly stretched infantry in the trench sections exposed to attack.

A sobering fact is that both officers and men of the 4th and 6th USCT involved in the attack were placing themselves in additional danger due to the Confederate policy toward African Americans in the Union Army, and those who commanded them. Due to harsh treatment of civilians after the Union capture of New Orleans by "Beast" Butler in April of 1862, he and the white officers serving under him were declared by Confederate authorities "not entitled to be considered as soldiers engaged in honorable warfare, but as robbers and criminals, deserving death; and that they and each of them be, whenever captured, reserved for execution" (quoted in Price 2011: 39). A further order went on to state that all African Americans captured while serving in the Union Army were "subject to death by the laws of every slave-holding State," and could not be recognized "in any way as soldiers subject to the rules of war" (quoted in Burkhardt 2007: 46). None of the above seems to have impaired the performance of the officers and men of the 4th and 6th USCT on September 29, 1864. The fact that they were likely to be killed if they surrendered probably encouraged them to fight with greater determination, and this remained the case with all African American troops for the remainder of the war.

To the battle-hardened Confederate infantrymen occupying the trenches at Chaffin's Farm/New Market Heights, the Union attack represented a massacre of the USCT troops. In total disregard of drill and training, the Texans and Arkansans climbed on top of the breastwork in front of their trenches during the attack in order to take better aim at the oncoming foe. Unaware of the fact that the African American infantrymen carried uncapped muskets and were unable to return fire, the defenders failed to appreciate the bravery of their adversaries and celebrated a momentary victory until forced to abandon their trenches by a further attack several hours later which forced them to fall back to the inner line of the Richmond defenses.

For the men of the Texas Brigade, yet another hard winter of campaigning lay ahead. To quote their chronicler J.B. Polley, "the Southern Confederacy lay in the throes of fast-approaching death" (Polley 1910: 269). With little duty to perform other than picketing the front line, time hung heavily upon their shoulders. Finally, following Pickett's defeat at Five Forks, the brigade abandoned their trenches with the rest of Lee's army on April 2, 1865. After serving as a rear-guard during the forced march which ended at Appomattox Court House, only 617 men of the original Texas Brigade of 5,353 surrendered to Grant's army on April 9, 1865.

ORDERS OF BATTLE

First Bull Run/Manassas, July 21, 1861

11th New York Infantry (1st Fire Zouaves)

Col Noah L. "Pony" Farnham (DOW), Lt Col John A. Cregier, and Maj Charles M. Leoser, plus eight staff consisting of one regimental quartermaster, one surgeon, one hospital steward, one chaplain (POW), one sergeant major, one quartermaster sergeant, one drum major, and one fife major, and 30 company-grade officers and 904 men = 945 all ranks. Casualties: 21 KIA, 28 WIA, 57 POW = 109.

Co. A (Right Flank Company): Capt John Coyle, 1/Lt Edward B. Knox, and Ensign Hugh S. Powers, plus 101 men. Casualties: 4 KIA, 1 WIA, 5 POW = 10.

Co. B: Capt Edward Byrnes, 1/Lt Stephen W. Stryker, and Ensign Cyrenus Harris, plus 97 men. Casualties: 1 KIA, 2 WIA, 3 POW = 6.

Co. C: Capt Michael C. Murphy (WIA), 1/Lt Louis Fitzgerald (WIA), and Ensign John A. Smith (WIA), plus 85 men. Casualties: 1 KIA, 3 WIA, 5 POW = 9.

Co. D: Capt John Downey (POW), 1/Lt Freeman Connor, and Ensign John Dowd, plus 90 men. Casualties: 5 KIA, 1 WIA, 6 POW inc. 1 WIA = 12.

Co. E (Color Company): Capt John B. "Jack" Leverich, 1/Lt William R.W. Chambers, and Ensign Lloyd W. Berry, plus 94 men. Casualties: 3 KIA, 1 WIA, 7 POW inc. 5 WIA = 11.

Co. F: Capt William H. Burns, 1/Lt Lucius S. Larrabee, and Ensign Jacob Wilsey, plus 84 men. Casualties: 2 KIA, 3 WIA, 7 POW inc. 2 WIA = 12.

Co. G: Capt Michael A. Tagan, 1/Lt Andrew M. Underhill (POW), and Ensign Daniel Divver (KIA), plus 92 men. Casualties: 1 WIA, 4 POW inc. 1 DOW = 5.

Co. H: Capt William Hackett, 1/Lt Joseph E. McFarland, and Ensign Patrick A. Gillan, and 85 men. Casualties: 2 KIA, 6 POW = 8.

Co. I: Capt John "Jack" Wildey, 1/Lt Edward Bernard, and Ensign James Nelson, plus 89 men. Casualties: 1 KIA, 4 WIA, 5 POW = 10.

Co. K (Left Flank Company): Capt Andrew D. Purtell, 1/Lt George H. Fergus, and Ensign John Matthews, plus 87 men. Casualties: 1 KIA, 1 WIA, 8 POW inc. 1 WIA = 10.

33rd Virginia Infantry

Col Arthur C. Cummings, Lt Col William Fitzhugh Lee (WIA), and Maj E.G. Lee, plus 23 company-grade officers and 560 men. Casualties: 37 KIA, 98 WIA, 8 MIA = 143. At First Bull Run/Manassas, this regiment was reduced to only eight companies, as Co. D and Co. I were on detached duty near Winchester, Virginia.

Co. A (Potomac Guards) (Right Flank Company): Capt Philip T. Grace, 1/Lt Simeon D. Long, and 2/Lt Jacob N. Buzzard, plus 51 men. Casualties: 4 KIA, 5 WIA = 9.

Co. B (Tom's Brook Guard): Capt Emanuel Crabill, 1/Lt Martin Strickler, and 2/Lt James H. Rosenberger (WIA), plus 65 men. Casualties: 4 KIA, 10 WIA, 1 MIA = 15.

Co. C (Tenth Legion Minute Men): Capt John Gatewood, 1/Lt Edward T. Miller (WIA), and 2/Lt John H. Grabill, plus 83 men. Casualties: 5 KIA, 16 WIA, 2 MIA = 23.

Co. E (Emerald Guard): Capt Marion M. Sibert (WIA), 1/Lt Thomas C. Fitzgerald (WIA), and 2/Lt John Ireland, plus 53 men. Casualties: 3 KIA, 11 WIA, 1 MIA = 15.

Co. F (Independent Greys or Hardy Greys): Capt Abraham Spengler, Lieutenant Aaron H. Wilson (WIA), plus 50 men. Casualties: 5 KIA, 8 WIA = 13.

Co. G (Mount Jackson Rifles): Capt George W. Allen, 1/Lt John L. Pitman, and 2/Lt Solomon K. Moore (WIA), plus 77 men. Casualties: 5 KIA, 16 WIA = 21.

Co. H (Page Greys): Capt William D. Rippetoe, 1/Lt William F. Hite (WIA), and 2/Lt Ambrose Shenk, plus 100 men. Casualties: 6 KIA, 15 WIA, 1 MIA = 22.

Co. K (Shenandoah Sharpshooters) (Left Flank Company): Capt David H. Walton, 1/Lt Levi Lutz, and 2/Lt Raphael Fadely, plus 81 men. Casualties: 5 KIA, 16 WIA, 3 MIA = 24.

"The Bloody Angle," Gettysburg, July 3, 1863

Union Second Division, II Corps (Brig Gen John Gibbon (WIA), Brig Gen William Harrow)

1st Brigade (Brig Gen William Harrow, Col Francis E. Heath): 19th Maine Infantry (Col Francis E. Heath (WIA), Lt Col Henry W. Cunningham), 15th Massachusetts Infantry (Lt Col George C. Joslin), 1st Minnesota Infantry (Capt Nathan S. Messick (KIA), Capt Henry C. Coates), 82nd New York Infantry (Capt John Darrow).

2nd Brigade (Brig Gen Alexander S. Webb (WIA), Col De Witt C. Baxter (WIA)): 69th Pennsylvania Infantry (Col Dennis O'Kane (KIA), Lt Col Martin Tschudy (KIA), Maj James M. Duffy (WIA), Capt William Davis), 71st Pennsylvania Infantry (Col Richard Penn Smith, Lt Col Charles Kochersperger), 72nd Pennsylvania Infantry (Col De Witt C. Baxter (WIA), Lt Col Theodore Hesser), 106th Pennsylvania Infantry (Lt Col William L. Curry)

3rd Brigade (Col Norman J. Hall): 19th Massachusetts Infantry (Col Arthur F. Devereux), 20th Massachusetts Infantry (Col Paul J. Revere (DOW), Lt Col George N. Macy (WIA), Capt Henry L. Abbott), 7th Michigan Infantry (Lt Col Amos E. Steele, Jr. (KIA), Maj Sylvanus W. Curtis), 42nd New York Infantry: (Col James E. Mallon), 59th New York Infantry: (Capt William McFadden; four companies only).

1st Massachusetts Sharpshooters Company (Capt William Plumer).

Battery A, 4th U.S Artillery (Lt Alonzo H. Cushing (KIA), 1/Sgt Frederick Füger; six 3in Rifles).

Battery A, 1st Rhode Island Light Artillery (Capt William A. Arnold; six 3in Rifles).

Pickett's Division (Maj Gen George E. Pickett)

Garnett's Brigade (Brig Gen Richard B. Garnett (KIA), Maj Charles S. Peyton): 8th Virginia Infantry (Col Eppa Hunton (WIA), Lt Col Norborne Berkeley (WIA & POW), Maj Edmund Berkeley (WIA)), 18th Virginia Infantry (Lt Col Henry A. Carrington (WIA & POW)), 19th Virginia Infantry (Col Henry Gantt (WIA), Lt Col John T. Ellis (DOW), Maj Charles S. Peyton), 28th Virginia Infantry (Col Robert C. Allen (KIA), Lt Col William Watts, Maj Nathaniel C. Wilson (DOW)), 56th Virginia Infantry (Col William D. Stuart (DOW), Lt Col Philip P. Slaughter).

Kemper's Brigade (Brig Gen James L. Kemper (WIA & POW), Col Joseph Mayo, Jr. (WIA)): 1st Virginia Infantry (Col Lewis B. Williams, Jr. (DOW), Maj Francis W. Langley (WIA)), 3rd Virginia Infantry (Col Joseph Mayo, Jr. (WIA); Lt Col Alexander D. Callcote (KIA), Maj William H. Pryor), 7th Virginia Infantry (Col Waller T. Patton (DOW), Lt Col C.C. Floweree), 11th Virginia Infantry (Maj Kirkwood Otey (WIA), Capt James R. Hutter (WIA & POW), Capt John Holmes Smith (WIA), Capt Albert W. Douthat), 24th Virginia Infantry (Col William R. Terry (WIA), Maj Joseph A. Hambrick (WIA), Capt William N. Bentley).

Armistead's Brigade (Brig Gen Lewis A. Armistead (DOW), Lt Col William White (WIA), Maj Joseph R. Cabell, Col William R. Aylett (WIA): 9th Virginia Infantry (Maj John C. Owens (DOW), Capt James J. Phillips), 14th Virginia Infantry (Col James G. Hodges (KIA), Lt Col William White (WIA), Maj Robert H. Poore (DOW)), 38th Virginia Infantry (Col Edward C. Edmonds (KIA), Lt Col Powatan B. Whittle (WIA), Maj Joseph R. Cabell), 53rd Virginia Infantry (Col William R. Aylett (WIA), Lt Col Rawley W. Martin (WIA & POW), Maj John C. Timberlake (POW), Capt Henry Edmunds), 57th Virginia Infantry (Col John B. Magruder (DOW), Lt Col Benjamin H. Wade (DOW), Maj Clement R. Fontaine (WIA)).

38th Virginia Light Artillery Battalion (Maj James Dearing): Fauquier (Virginia) Artillery Battery (Capt Robert M. Stribling; two 20-pdr Parrotts, four Napoleons), Hampton (Virginia) Artillery Battery (Capt William H. Caskie; one 10-pdr Parrott, one 3in Rifle, two Napoleons), Richmond (Virginia) Fayette Artillery Battery (Capt Miles C. Macon; two 10-pdr Parrotts, two Napoleons), Blount's (Virginia) Artillery Battery (Capt Joseph G. Blount; four Napoleons).

Chaffin's Farm/New Market Heights, September 29, 1864

Union Third Division, XVIII Corps (Brig Gen Charles J. Paine)

1st Brigade (Col John H. Holman): 1st USCT (not known), 22nd USCT (Col Joseph B. Kiddoo), 37th USCT (Lt Col Abiel G. Chamberlain; eight companies only).

2nd Brigade (Col Alonzo G. Draper): 5th USCT (Lt Col Giles W. Shurtleff), 36th USCT (Lt Col Benjamin F. Pratt), 38th USCT (Lt Col Dexter E. Clapp).

3rd Brigade (Col Samuel A. Duncan (WIA); Col John W. Ames): 4th USCT (Major Augustus S. Boernstein), 6th USCT (Col John W. Ames).

The Texas Brigade (Lt Col Frederick Bass)

3rd Arkansas Infantry: Lt Col Robert S. Taylor

1st Texas Infantry: not known

4th Texas Infantry: Lt Col Clinton M. Winkler

5th Texas Infantry: Capt Tacitus T. Clay

SELECT BIBLIOGRAPHY

Anonymous (1861). *A Manual of the Piece adopted to the Rifle Musket, The Rifle, and Other Infantry Arms.* Louisville, KY: J.W. Tompkins & Co.

Abbott, Stephen G. (1890). *The First Regiment New Hampshire Volunteers in the Great Rebellion.* Keene, NH: Sentinel Printing Co.

Bates, Samuel P. (1868–71). *History of the Pennsylvania Volunteers, 1861–1865,* 5 vols. Harrisburg, PA: B. Singerly, State Printer.

Beidelman, George Washington, ed. Catherine H. Vanderslice (1978). *The Civil War Letters of George Washington Beidelman.* New York, NY: Vantage Press, Inc.

Beyer, W.F., & O.F. Keydel, eds (1905). *Deeds of Valor, Vol. 1.* Detroit, MI: Perrien-Keydel Co.

Bull Runnings: A Journal of the Digitization of a Civil War Battle. http://bullrunnings.wordpress.com/ (accessed January 29, 2013).

Burkhardt, George S. (2007). *Confederate Rage, Yankee Wrath: No Quarter in the Civil War.* Carbondale, IL: Southern Illinois University Press.

Cary, Lt Col Richard M. (1861). *Skirmishers' Drill and Bayonet Exercise.* Richmond, VA: West & Johnston Publishers.

Casey, Maj Gen Silas (1862). *Infantry Tactics for the Instruction, Exercise, and Manoeuvres of the Soldier, A Company, Line of Skirmishers, Battalion, Brigade, or Corps de Armee* (three vols). New York, NY: D. Van Nostrand.)

Casey, Maj Gen Silas (1863). *Infantry Tactics for the Instruction, Exercise, and Manoeuvres of the Soldier, A Company, Line of Skirmishers, Battalion for the use of The Colored Troops of the United States Infantry.* New York, NY: D. Van Nostrand.

Casler, John O. (1971). *John O. Casler's Four Years in the Stonewall Brigade,* 3rd Edition. Dayton, OH: Morningside Bookshop.

Coulter, E. Merton (1950. *A History of the South, Vol. VII: The Confederate States of America 1861–1865,* Baton Rouge, LA: Louisiana State University Press.

Eby, Jr., Cecil D. (1961). *Diaries of Daniel Hunter Strother: A Virginia Yankee in the Civil War.* Chapel Hill, NC: University of North Carolina Press.

Ellsworth, Elmer E. (1861). *The Zouave Drill, being a Complete Manual of Arms for the use of The Rifled Musket.* Philadelphia, PA: T.B. Peterson & Brothers.

Frinkle Fry (pseudonymn for Elnathan B. Tyler) (1872). *Wooden Nutmegs at Bull Run:* A Humorous Account of some of the Exploits and Experiences of the Three Months Connecticut Brigade. Hartford, CT: George L. Coburn, Steam Print.

Gilham, Maj William (1861). *Manual of Instruction for the Volunteers and Militia of the United States.* Philadelphia, PA: Charles DeSilver.

Griffith, Paddy (1986). *Battle in the Civil War: Generalship and Tactics in America 1861–65.* Camberley: Fieldbooks.

Griffith, Paddy (1987). *Rally Once Again: Battle Tactics of the American Civil War.* Marlborough: The Crowood Press.

Hardee, Bvt Lt William J. (1855). *Rifle and Light Infantry Tactics for the Exercise and Manoeuvres of Troops when acting as Light Infantry or Riflemen* (two vols). Philadelphia, PA: Lippincott, Grambo & Co.

Haskell, Frank Aretas (1908). *The Battle of Gettysburg.* Boston, MA: Commandery of the State of Massachusetts, Military Order of the Loyal Legion of the United States.

Hassler, Warren W. (1970). *The First Day at Gettysburg: Crisis at the Crossroads.* Tuscaloosa, AL: University of Alabama Press.

Hewett, Janet B. (1994–2001). *Supplement to the Official Records of the Union and Confederate Armies* (100 vols). Wilmington, NC: Broadfoot Publishing Co.

Jones, A.C. (1917). "Texas and Arkansas at Fort Harrison," *Confederate Veteran Magazine*, Vol. 25, No. 1, January 1917. Nashville, TN: S.A. Cunningham, 24-25.

Katcher, Philip (1992). *The American Civil War Source Book.* London: Arms & Armour Press.

Lanning, Michael Lee (2006). *The Civil War 100.* Naperville, IL: Sourcebooks, Inc.

Lash, Gary G. (2001). *"Duty Well Done": The History of Edward Baker's California Regiment (71st Pennsylvania Infantry).* Baltimore, MD: Butternut and Blue.

Lee, Capt James Kendall (1860). *The Volunteer's Handbook containing an Abridgement of Hardee's Infantry Tactics.* Richmond, VA: West & Johnston.

Longacre, Edward G. (2003). *A Regiment of Slaves: The 4th United States Colored Infantry, 1863–1866.* Mechanicsburg, PA: Stackpole Books.

Patterson, Robert (1865). *A Narrative of the Campaign in the Valley of the Shenandoah, in 1861.* Philadelphia, PA: John Campbell.

Pohanka, Brian C., & Patrick A. Schroeder (2011). *With the 11th New York Fire Zouaves In Camp, Battle, and Prison.* Lynchburg, VA: Schroeder Publications.

Polley, J.B. (1910). *Hood's Texas Brigade: Its Marches, its Battles, its Achievements.* New York, NY: Neale Publishing Co.

Price, James S. (2011). *The Battle of New Market Heights: Freedom will be Theirs by the Sword.* Charleston, SC: The History Press.

Reidenbaugh, Lowell (1987). *33rd Virginia Infantry,* The Virginia Regimental History Series. Lynchburg, VA: H.E. Howard, Inc.

Rollins, Richard, ed. (2005). *Pickett's Charge: Eyewitness Accounts at the Battle of Gettysburg.* Mechanicsburg, PA: Stackpole Books.

Scott, Robert N. (1880–1901). *Official Records of the War of the Rebellion* (127 vols). Washington, DC: Government Printing Office.

Scott, Winfield (1835). *Infantry Tactics or Rules for the Exercise and Manoeuvres of the United States Infantry* (three vols). New York, NY: George Dearborn Publisher.

Sears, Stephen W. (1992). *To the Gates of Richmond: The Peninsula Campaign.* New York, NY: First Mariner Books.

Strother, David H., ed. Cecil Eby, Jr. (1961).*A Virginia Yankee in the Civil War: The Diaries of David Hunter Strother.* Chapel Hill, NC: University of North Carolina Press.

The Sable Arm: A Blog Dedicated to the United States Colored Troops of the Civil War Era. http://sablearm.blogspot.co.uk/2011_07_01_archive.html (accessed January 29, 2013).

"Tiger! Zouave!!" http://myrtle-avenue.com/firezou/ (accessed January 29, 2013).

Tsouras, Peter G., ed. (1992). *The Book of Military Quotations.* St. Paul, MN: Zenith Press.

Williams, George W. (1888). *A History of the Negro Troops in the War of the Rebellion 1861–65.* New York, NY: Harper & Brothers.

Winkler, Angelina V. (1894). *The Confederate Capital & Hood's Texas Brigade.* Austin, TX: E. Von Boeckmann.

Young, William A., & Patricia C. Young (2009). *History of the 56th Virginia Infantry Regiment* (2nd Edition). Fort Walton Beach, FL: James Keir Baughman.

Plus various newspapers and journals including:

Boston Daily Advertiser, MA (*BDA*); *Buffalo Evening News,* NY (*BEN*); *Cleveland Morning Leader,* OH (*CML*); *Columbus Daily Times,* GA (*CDT*); *Confederate Veteran* (*CV*), *Hartford Daily Courant,* CT (*HDC*); *Lewiston Daily Evening Journal,* ME (*LDEJ*), *Milwaukee Daily Sentinel,* WI (*MDS*); *New Hampshire Statesman,* Concord, NH (*NHS*); *New-York Evening Post* (*NYEP*); *New York Herald* (*NYH*); *New York Times* (*NYT*); *Philadelphia Inquirer,* PA (*PI*); *Richmond Dispatch,* VA (*RD*); *Shenandoah Herald,* VA, via http://www.vagenweb.org/shenandoah/wars/civil/grabill-diary.html (accessed January 30, 2013) (*SH*); *The Golden Era,* San Francisco (*TGE*); *Times-Dispatch,* Richmond, VA, via http://www.findagrave.com/cgi-bin/fg.cgi?page=gr&GRid=7171054 (accessed January 30, 2013) (*TD*);*Tri-Weekly Southern Guardian,* Columbia, SC (*TWSG*).

INDEX